The Michmash Miracles

How Old Testament History Helped the British in World War 1

NIGEL MESSENGER

Published by Nigel Messenger in 2021

ISBN 978-1-8383569-2-7

Book Cover Design and Typeset by The Daydream Academy, Stroud, Gloucestershire.

CONTENTS

INTRODUCTION

How Old Testament history helped the British win a battle in World War I. Based on the incredible true story of two battles three thousand years apart.

The first battle was recorded in Samuel in the Old Testament, where the Israelites were facing a huge Philistine Army on a mountain near the village of Michmash. Jonathan, King Saul's son, finds a secret path to reach and outflank the enemy, and eventually wins an extraordinary victory.

The second battle takes places in 1918 when the British Army is facing the Ottomans in the same place and in similar circumstances. A British officer is reading the Bible the night before the battle and finds the reference to Michmash. He learns about the tactics Jonathan used three thousand years before and the secret path he found. Using similar tactics, he and his men win a magnificent victory over the Ottomans.

Book One - Jonathan

Chapter 1

The Chase

The boy was running for his life; he had been running for around three hours and was trying to keep ahead of his pursuers and their hunting dogs. Pounding hard on the stony ground, he was thankful they had let him wear his heavy-based leather sandals which were firmly strapped up to his knees, otherwise his feet would have been torn to shreds and he would have been forced to give up.

The boy was small for his age, but stocky with a strong build and well-muscled legs. His head was a mass of curls which bounced as he ran. If the situation had not been so serious, he might have seemed almost comical to an onlooker.

They were not far behind now. He could hear his heart beating loudly while he tried to control his breathing, but this was getting harder. Painfully aware that his body was dehydrating, he was gasping and sweat was soaking his head and body, his need for water becoming serious.

He knew he could not go on much longer. The hunters were getting closer. He was desperately trying to think ahead and work out how this would end, but his mind was focussed on keeping going and getting ahead of the men and their vicious dogs. He was running in the heart of the hilly area of central Palestine, which made the race tough and exhausting. Hopefully, this was also true for his pursuers.

Then he saw his opportunity: a steep cliff rising to his left. If he climbed high enough, the dogs could not follow him, but he was sure a couple of the men would still go after him. The others would have to stay behind with the dogs and find a longer way round.

He reached the steepest part of the cliff on top of the slope and knew he could climb it with relative ease. The men and dogs were only a few paces behind him, and he could hear their rising excitement as they were getting closer to their prey. He stopped for a heartbeat and drew breath with a rough gasp, then stepped up to the first foothold to start his climb onto the honey-coloured rock.

It was an easy climb to start with, but he was weakened after the long chase. The men had untied the leashes and the three dogs reached the foot of the cliff in an instant. They were leaping high, one after the other, to snap at his ankles. Their yelps and snarls terrified him and the thought of being attacked and savaged by the dogs was his worst nightmare. He was shaking with horror, but fortunately, was just out of reach of their slavering jaws. He climbed higher, well away from the monsters.

Looking down, he saw that there were five men in total who had all stopped to recover their breathing, wasting precious moments drinking from their water flasks. This was the first time he had had the opportunity to observe them: wearing scant clothing, they had dark brown skin and looked like the Nubian slaves he had seen at the slave market. He knew that they had been chosen because of their superior running skills, and although their bodies were shiny with sweat, they could run fast all day.

Two of the men started climbing below him, but he had reached the top of the cliff. He had to stop them before they killed him. Picking up a large, heavy stone, he lobbed it over the side of the cliff, aiming at the leading climber.

He was accurate with his first shot. It hit the Nubian on his right shoulder with sufficient force to knock him off his hold, sending him hurtling towards the ground some twenty paces below. The man fell awkwardly and did not move. His comrades rushed to his side to help him.

The boy lobbed three more stones at the second man as he was climbing up, but he did not hit him. The man looked up at him steadfastly and moved sideways at the last minute when the stone was dropping towards him, slowly reaching the summit without harm. All the boy had to defend himself with was a short wooden sword, given to him by Abner's men as they roared with laughter. It was more like a child's toy.

He was not expected to survive this chase.

The Nubian man had a long, thin dagger at his waist. The wooden sword was the boy's only option.

As the man reached the top of the cliff and stood upright with his dagger drawn, the boy ran at him with his wooden weapon raised. The man stepped aside, and the boy only just avoided falling over the edge. The man lunged at him with his dagger and cut into his tunic; the boy stepped back, knowing that he was now fighting for his life.

The man lunged again, and this time, the boy easily avoided the blade. It was in this moment that he realised his fighting training was vastly superior to this man's, and for the first time, he was grateful for the harsh lessons given to him by Abner.

He brought his wooden sword down hard on his attacker's wrist and the man cried out in pain as the bronze dagger fell from his hand. The boy now had the advantage and lunged at his stomach, stabbing him, the sharp point of his wooden sword penetrating the skin. The pain caused the man to step back and totter dangerously on the edge of the cliff. The boy gave him a gentle shove and, with a piercing scream, he fell to certain death.

The boy was gaining the advantage over his pursuers. It would take the remaining three of them some time to circle around the cliff with their dogs and find him. He desperately needed a drink and looked at the receding slope, heading towards an area of green vegetation and trees in the hope of finding a spring. He did not recognise the landscape, but judged that he was heading towards a safety zone.

After a short run, he found a fast-flowing stream and fell into it, drinking deeply and gratefully. His body was so seriously dehydrated by this time, he wondered whether he would ever stop drinking, but he finally gasped and fell back on to the bank, giving thanks for the wonderful relief.

The stream was just deep enough to hide his body. He jumped in and tore out several reeds. Dipping his head under the water, he put the reeds between his lips and drew the air from above into his lungs, keeping as still as possible and allowing the movement of the water and the thickly growing plants to obscure his body.

After a few moments, he could make out the forms of his pursuers as they stopped to look for him. They fell down to guzzle some much-needed water and he was afraid that they would see him. Fortunately, he was well hidden by the mass of reeds, but he was getting uncomfortable and desperate to move. His body was cooling rapidly, which initially was a huge relief, but was now making him suffer extreme stiffness.

As he started to shake uncontrollably, he saw the men move away. He waited for as long as he could, and then slowly stood up and stepped out of the stream.

Too late, he saw that one of the Nubians had stopped. No more than twenty paces away, facing him, the Nubian started moving towards him and the boy turned and ran in the opposite direction. While he was running, he reached for the sling which was tied to his belt and pulled it free. Still running, he ducked down and picked up a stone, loaded it, turned around and flung it with all his strength. He'd had plenty of practice doing this.

The stone thwacked into the Nubian's shoulder and the man yelped with the intense pain. Staggering, he just about held his balance and kept running forward as the boy was loading his second stone. Again, he turned and swung the sling towards his pursuer. The Nubian ducked and the stone whistled harmlessly over his head.

The Nubian was gaining ground and was only about ten paces behind the boy when he swung the sling for the third time. This time, the stone landed on his pursuer's forehead with a loud crack and forced his head back sharply. His legs gave way, and he was dead before his body reached the ground.

The boy moved as quickly as he could, stealing the dead man's dagger and running back to the stream to drink several more deep draughts of the cool water. He then set off, running in the opposite direction from his pursuers.

***

The lion was lying very still in the shade of a large rock, his dark golden-brown fur blending in with the sandy soil. He had not eaten for several days and was weak with hunger; he would die soon if he could not find some fresh meat. His eyelids started to fall in his debilitated state, and in moments, he was sleeping.

He woke up suddenly as a figure ran past him. Now fully alert, he watched as two men with three dogs ran along the path by his rock. He charged out of his lair and went straight for the dogs, crushing the first to the ground with his heavy paws before sideswiping the other two. They were killed instantly.

The Nubian nearest him shrieked in terror, dropping the dogs' leads and running back the way he had come. In three bounds, the lion caught up with him, raised his paws and lacerated his back with terrible ferocity. The man crashed to the ground and the air was forced out of his body. The lion opened his massive mouth, exposing his teeth, and crushed the man's head instantly.

The second Nubian carried on running at twice his previous speed. Further ahead, the boy turned round to assess the situation, relieved that he had not been the one to disturb the lion as he ran past. The boy had never seen a lion before as they were rare in these parts. He had studied drawings, but never imagined that the beast would be so massive and frightening. Would his sling be effective on this huge, terrifying creature?

Horrified, he watched as the lion bit into his victim, satisfying his extreme hunger and lingering over his meal, lapping up the man's blood and gouging out his meat and delicious entrails. Having seen more than enough, the boy and the surviving man then ran as fast as they could away from the lion, praying that the beast would be satisfied with his catch. They were almost four hundred paces away from the lion when he roared.

The boy stopped and turned around to assess his chances and options. Abner had constantly told him to be cool and calm and think positively in the face of danger. All the same, he was pleased that there were two of them; the remaining Nubian was now an ally against a common enemy.

The light was beginning to fade and shadows were lengthening. The lion emitted a most terrible noise, a primal scream which shook the earth and the air around them. Terrified, the boy thought for a moment he was going to lose control over his guts as the noise seemed to penetrate right through to his soul.

He had never had to face a situation like this before. The lion was enormous and frightening, but in the extreme tension of the moment, he had a regal dignity about him. A short curly mane surrounding his massive head, he moved forward rapidly on his huge pads, gaining immense speed almost instantly. The new allies ran towards higher ground in an almost hopeless attempt to get to safety, but the lion was gaining on them fast, bounding upwards without difficulty.

The boy closed his eyes for a fraction of a second and wished that this awful event was not happening. Imagining himself relaxing at home in safety, he then snapped out of his reverie and grabbed a fist-sized stone from the ground. Without losing any pace, he placed it into his sling.

He turned quickly and hurled the stone as hard as he could, using every muscle in his body to maximum effect. The stone hit the lion in his shoulder, and he roared in pain, coming to an abrupt stop and kicking up clouds of dust as he did so. The boy reloaded as fast as he could and slung his second stone. Hitting the lion on the back, it bounced off vertically. Again, the lion roared. He was limping in agony and had slowed down to a walk.

The boy ran to catch up with the Nubian as the lion ran after both of them, but more slowly now, his wounds causing him to limp painfully and trail a trickle of blood. Man and boy shouted ideas at each other, and then reached a joint decision: they each picked up a huge rock and, turning, hurled them at the lion. They repeated this bombardment, some of the rocks hitting the lion and slowing him down. The boy screamed to the man to keep throwing as he drew his knife and, with extraordinary bravery, walked towards the wounded lion.

The lion came towards the boy and rather feebly jumped up at him. Skilfully stepping aside, the boy brought the knife down into the back of the lion's neck. As the lion collapsed, he stuck out a paw and lacerated the boy's chest, but his strength had gone and he fell onto his side, crashing into the boy's body, knocking him over with a horrible crushing and crunching sound.

The boy was only just conscious, but he was still alive. The irony of him facing and killing a lion, considering the nickname his own curly mane, along with the ingenuity and courage he had shown from an early age, had earned him, didn't even cross his mind. He was merely an exhausted boy with no idea that he would go on to achievements so extraordinary that they would be told and retold by people all over the world, even after several millennia.

Chapter 2

Happy Early Days

The sun was at its zenith now, but from his position on the high side of the pass, Jonathan could enjoy the cooling breeze wafting over the elevated ground. There was little greenery, apart from a few scattered fir trees trying to break up the harsh landscape. He was lying on his front, peering over the edge as he waited for the arrival of the men.

He watched an eagle flying low in the sky, coasting with majestic ease and slowly climbing on the warm air, its brown feathered wings spread as wide as a blanket. There was a long wriggling snake in its beak and Jonathan liked to think this was a good omen for the forthcoming day, for this was his first opportunity to show his father that he was worthy of the command and the faith the man had placed in him.

But for now, Jonathan had a few moments to reflect on his life so far and how he had come to be here, lying on this craggy rock.

***

Jonathan's father Saul, with his great physical and spiritual presence, had been the popular choice to become King and unite the twelve tribes of Israel, protecting them against their fierce neighbours, particularly the Philistines. Under pressure from his people, Samuel, the High Priest, had anointed Saul reluctantly, believing that God did not want a King for Israel and fearing that the Israelites would lose some power as a result.

From a very young age, Jonathan had known that his father was mentally unstable. When Jonathan was a little boy, Saul would whip him with alarming, and painful, regularity, and he would run to Samuel for shelter and protection. He could even recall his father throwing a spear at him because he had dared to disagree with him. Luckily, the spear had missed its target – narrowly – and Jonathan had run out of the tent and left his father to cool down for a couple of days.

Because his attempts to score a victory over the Philistines had been unsuccessful, Saul's moods had become worse. Sometimes, he would froth at the mouth in his rage, and then everyone was terrified to go anywhere near him. Jonathan had been there when his father had killed an unfortunate slave for no particular reason, and there was no doubt in his young mind that his father was insane. Even Samuel, the Priest who had anointed and crowned Saul, was increasingly losing patience, his confidence in the people's chosen one dwindling as he regretted his decision more and more.

However, despite Saul's raging temper, Jonathan had very warm memories of his early childhood at home in Gibeah with his mother Ahinoam. He could still remember the sights and the smells of her cooking and how he could hardly wait to eat her divine offerings. She baked bread every morning, mixing flour, water and olive oil, kneading the dough, and then pressing it out ready for cooking on top of the stove, and it was wonderful to wake up to the delicious aroma wafting up to his bedroom. The lovely smell would fill the house and draw him to the kitchen to steal a morsel. And it would be ready in no time at all — such a simple process with such delicious and satisfying results.

His favourite dish was lamb stew, simmered for several days with fruits, herbs and spices. Ahinoam also made a delicious fish dish with a white wine sauce, and he loved her chicken roasted in a hot fire or steeped in tasty juices and cooked slowly on top of the stove. Another favourite was goat cooked in hot spices.

She would bake the most delicious cakes, pouring honey over them, and he thoroughly enjoyed the fresh fruits his mother cut up and mixed with juices and cream on top. Sometimes, he just could not get enough to eat as he had an enormous appetite while he was growing noticeably on a daily basis. The only thing he disliked intensely was milk, which she made him drink every day. He vowed he would never touch the stuff again when he became an adult.

Jonathan had several much younger brothers and sisters, but the age gap between them was so large, they were uninteresting to him. They were little more than babies when he left home.

The family lived in a big two-storey house. His grandfather Kish had built the house in stone with a cypress and pine frame many years ago, and although it was small considering the importance of the family and definitely not a palace, it was the largest home in Gibeah. Jonathan still loved the house, even though it was cold and draughty in the winter, as he'd had a very happy upbringing there.

His father rarely came to the house and the whole family was pleased about this. On the odd occasion he did visit, he always caused huge disruption, and

Jonathan suspected that his mother would rather Saul had stayed away permanently.

Jonathan would accompany his mother to the local market, sometimes with his friend Adam, where she bought food and household items. The boys loved the sights, sounds and smells. There were hundreds of stalls, some with colourful spices and seeds, such as mustard, chilli, myrrh, cinnamon, saffron, cumin, salt, garlic, and others with a kaleidoscope of coloured cloths from places like Egypt and Babylon decorated with Arab embroidery, carved olive-wood toys and ornaments, trinkets and jewellery, brightly coloured stones, and gold and silver. There were many varieties of breads, including unleavened, along with flour and soft, sweet fruits. The temptation to take a peach, an apple, a date, or some grapes was almost overwhelming. There were also figs, melons, black and green olives, and other stalls held beans, cucumbers, leeks and onions. Goat, lamb, beef and deer meats were on sale, and some stalls offered quails, chickens and pigeons. The many different kinds of fish had to be sold before midday, otherwise the heat would cause them to smell strongly and put the buyers off. There were always queues for the olive oil, vinegar and wines, but of course, the honey was everyone's favourite.

His mother loved to try the heady perfumes, made from the flowers which covered the hills after rainfall, and look over stalls of woollen and linen dresses and light shawls, buying expensive oils and make-up for her eyes and lips. Jonathan knew that the curvy pots with beautifully painted designs made from various metals were Greek in origin, but wondered if they had been made by his people's enemies. The Philistines had originally come from that part of the world.

He loved to listen to the sounds of the market: the shouts of the traders, the music of the lyre and drums, the beautiful singing of young boys and girls, and the agonised murmurs of the beggars. Live animals were everywhere: goats, sheep and chickens adding to the clamour as they were hawked to potential buyers. The camels and donkeys for carrying the many goods were particularly vocal. Shouts, arguments and haggling competed with the music played by small bands of men, sitting together on the ground. There were many different instruments: pipes, bells, cymbals and flutes, but Jonathan's favourite was the sound of the harp, which mesmerised him.

One man would play a flute on his own, fascinating the crowd with his ability to entice a snake to rise up out of a basket. The onlookers would throw some coins towards him, and then escape rapidly before the snake came after them.

The warm aroma of spices and bread, the smell of fresh fish and meat, burning incense and perfumes overlay the less pleasant smells of animals. The acrid scent of lamb, ox, camel and horse dung pervaded the air, but it merely added to the rich atmosphere and ambience of the market.

One of the traders attracted a crowd of people by hawking magical remedies for all kinds of ailments. He said he could cure hives, stiffened bones, plague and even had the secret for everlasting life. Few believed him, but an occasional passer-by bought his medicines in the hope of curing some long-term malady.

The beggars intrigued the boys. One skinny old man pleading for money was rumoured to be older than the Patriarch, Abraham – well, that's what Jonathan's friend Adam told him, and of course, Jonathan believed him. This man was so old, he no longer had any eyes. Interspersed with the elderly and the infirm were wretched young children begging, some with badly crippled arms and legs. The boys always felt sorry for them and spilled a few coins on their laps.

The boys especially loved the magicians, one of whom could produce a beautiful dove out of thin air. Another could make objects disappear. He would persuade someone in his audience to give up a valuable object such as a ring, which would vanish, and then miraculously reappear behind a boy's ear.

A group of men were often playing some kind of gambling game with dice and Jonathan saw piles of coins on the table. He wondered how this game worked. Other men played an incomprehensible game on a black and white board with soldiers and horses facing each other. He and Adam would have liked to learn more about this, but they didn't want to disturb the players by asking.

Hundreds of people of all types from all lands flocked to the market. The skin tones went through every shade, from the people of Africa whose skin was almost black to those with yellow hair and pale skin from the cold lands in the north, many months' travel from Jonathan's homeland. Some people had eyes that looked as if they were half closed, but the boys did not know where they were from. There were old men with long beards, women in beautifully coloured clothes, frowning priests and holy men who stood on orange boxes and preached sermons about the God of Israel, and many excited children.

Jonathan and Adam got their first sighting of a leper at the market. These unfortunate people were normally forced to stay in their own colonies due to their highly infectious condition. It had no cure, which meant many were terrified of them. Some thought that they would suffer the same affliction just by looking at them. The man the boys saw had horrible skin on his face that looked as if it was melting and sightless eyes. Jonathan and Adam felt helpless and terribly sorry for him.

Looking beyond the market, Jonathan loved the views of the small white houses which covered the surrounding hills and seemed to sparkle in the sun, and the big ornate buildings belonging to the Priests and their rulers.

***

Every day, Jonathan and his friends had to attend school with the Priests. Then, after a short siesta in the heat of the day, they would play outside, fighting with wooden swords, climbing cliffs and trees, skipping, hunting birds and rabbits with slings and bows, and running races on foot or horseback. When the weather was bad, they had to stay in the Temple and play board games.

Jonathan clearly remembered his long days of learning at the Temple in Gibeah. He loved sitting on the cool marble benches with his friends, listening to the Priests, especially the High Priest and Judge Samuel, telling them how the great Leader Moses had brought their people out of Egypt in the hot lands to the south and saved them from terrible oppression under their slave masters. Guided by God, Moses had led them to Canaan, the land He had promised to them, the land flowing with milk and honey. The Red Sea had miraculously parted to allow them to escape their captors, and then the waves had come together to destroy their enemies in their chariots. The boys learned how Moses had brought down the tablets of stone etched with God's commandments and Torah scrolls teaching His people how to live their lives.

Samuel was a man of God and the people believed that God spoke through him. He instructed Jonathan in religious practices and told him that he must have faith in God who had chosen the Israelites as His favoured people. Samuel was the oldest man Jonathan knew, and his whiskery face was heavily lined and shrunken, the loose brown skin reminding Jonathan of a walnut. He had a strange high-pitched voice, but he was kind and patient as he spent hours instructing the youngsters about the Ark of the Covenant.

"The Ark was carried by the Israelite people on their journeys all those years ago," Samuel explained.

"Can I see it?" Jonathan asked.

"Next week, I want you to come with me to Shiloh, a very holy place of worship. I will show it to you, but only for a few minutes. You must understand that this is a great privilege for you."

Samuel was as good as his word. Jonathan was startled by the experience of seeing the Ark for the first time.

"I can't believe how small it is. Who made the Ark?"

"No one is too sure, but what we do know is that it's God's design. It's made of acacia wood covered in gold."

"It's no bigger than my mother's linen box."

Jonathan gazed in awe at the dazzling beauty before him. The rich gold moulding all around the wooden box-like structure was startling; there was an angelic baby with wings on the top and the box had intricate feet.

"This is the most sacred symbol of our people and it has a tremendous power over our enemies," Samuel explained. "The Ark has enabled us to win our wars. Once, when the Philistines captured the Ark, it caused them to suffer diseases and pestilence and so much distress, they sent it back!"

"Can I see inside?"

"Absolutely not!" Samuel replied firmly. He went on to explain how the Ark contained the stone tablets on to which God had etched the Ten Commandments on Mount Sinai. Moses had then brought the tablets down to the people. They explained the rules of living a good and just life, and now Samuel was tasked with guarding them and the Ark closely. No one else was allowed to see either without his permission.

"The Ark is the most precious possession of our people and we believe that it empowers us in our struggles. It has inspired our armies and generals for generations. And do you know who was the greatest general of them all?"

"Gideon? Or Joshua?" Jonathan asked.

"No, the greatest of them all was a woman. Any ideas?"

Jonathan shook his head, confused.

"She was called Deborah. A Judge and Prophet, she was known as the Mother of Israel, and she won a significant victory over the Canaanites. Predicting when the rains would come, she tricked them into attacking our army by the River of Kishon, and the resultant floods disabled the enemy's nine hundred chariots. Her victory ensured an unprecedented forty years of peace."

"Who were these Canaanites?"

"The Canaanites were a nation advanced in art, architecture, trade and education, and we have now absorbed much of their culture. They lived in the northern part of our country and were more deadly enemies than the Philistines are now. They threatened to annihilate us."

Intrigued, Jonathan learned about the mighty Samson who had defeated the Philistines. The man possessed immense strength and had died a hero when, after having been blinded by the Philistines, he shook the pillars of their palace, causing the whole building to collapse. Many Philistines had perished with him. Jonathan learned about

Othniel, Gideon and Ehud who had fought enemies such as the Amalekites and Midianites, and of course the famous general Joshua who had successfully attacked Jericho. At a blast from his trumpets, the walls had collapsed.

"How on earth could a trumpet have crumbled the walls? That's impossible!"

"Well, first of all, Jonathan, with God by our side, nothing is impossible. But in this case, there were some other factors involved. The walls were in a perilous condition already, and the tremors caused by the marching weakened them still further. The tremendous noise from the trumpets simply finished the job."

"Why were some Judges and Prophets so successful in battles and wars and as leaders of our people, while others were not?"

"You mentioned Gideon before," Samuel replied. "He was successful because he was a true prophet and didn't worship false gods and idols. He worshipped the one true God, and because of this, God helped him in his endeavours."

"But what did Gideon achieve, making him so successful?"

"After Deborah had promoted peace and prosperity in Israel for forty years, the people turned against God and worshipped idols instead. They even built an altar to Baal."

Jonathan shivered at the mention of Baal's name. The Israelites were told he was an evil spirit.

"God visited Gideon dressed as a traveller and performed a miracle to prove who He was."

"What was the miracle?" Jonathan asked.

"He caused a huge flame to flare out of a rock. He then instructed Gideon to destroy the altar of the false gods.

"Gideon had a huge army of over 30,000 men and God instructed him to send home those who were afraid to face their enemies. Only 10,000 remained. God then told Gideon to take these men to the lake to drink water. Most of the men used their hands to scoop up the water, but a few put their mouths to the lake to lap like dogs. God deemed the former to be cowards and ordered Gideon to send them home. Then, a mere 300 remained.

"With this small force and God's help, Gideon managed to overcome the huge army of the Midianites. On God's instruction, he gave each man a trumpet and a torch, thereby tricking the enemy into believing that a huge force was attacking them.

"After his victory, Gideon refused to be called King, stating that only God was the ruler of the people. But he managed to bring about forty years of peace, as Deborah had done, before the idolaters took over once again."

One of the important duties of the Priests, Samuel told Jonathan and his friends, was to record the history of their people, and they wrote a new paper each year. There was now a huge record written on papyrus, stretching back to the time of Abraham, including the years the Israelites had been held in captivity in Egypt. The priests ensured that the annual summary was secured in a cave near to the Salt Sea known only to them, sealed in jars so the original papers would not be damaged by weather or insects. There were copies in the Temple for teaching purposes.

"You must know your history. Every boy and girl must learn from these archives about their ancestors. Know and remember their achievements and the developments of our people. Learn how our beliefs and customs were formed.

"I cannot stress how important this is. If we do not know our history, we cannot know how to plan for the future. Our history tells us what we must do, what works and what God expects from us. If our history is not written down with the strictest accuracy, false gods will come and tell us lies about the past. There are, of course, episodes in our history which we may not be too proud of, but we must remember and understand them so that we won't repeat the mistakes of the past.

"You will all read and learn your history from our archives, and we Priests will check your knowledge."

The students, of course, were not happy about this as they knew how long the work would take. Adam was the first to respond.

"We cannot be expected to learn everything about our history. It's too much."

"Yes, it will take a long time, but we will spend four hours every day reading and learning. There will be tests periodically and no one will be excused. There is nothing more important for your development than this."

The boys got tired of Samuel saying the same thing each day: "If you don't know where you've come from, you won't know where you are going", but there was no more argument. They knew Samuel would not allow dissent. Gradually, they began to understand the importance of this vital subject.

***

Jonathan and his friends couldn't wait to get out of the Temple each day and play. Most of all, they loved to swim in the lake to cool off when it was hot. Fishing was another favourite pastime, and when they were successful, they were proud to take their catch home. But they didn't catch much. They used primitive sticks and hooks, and the fish usually evaded them easily.

One day, a fishing boat came into land near them and the three fishermen gave the boys some of the catch from their nets as they had had a good day on the lake. The boys' mothers were delighted!

Jonathan became very good at climbing and loved scaling the heights around his childhood home at Gibeah. As a young boy, he practised with his friends on a dozen different climbs and was always looking for new challenges, and slowly, he improved.

One of the climbs involved finding a way over a huge overhang that could only be conquered using finger grips. Jonathan's friend, Ishmael, was dared by the other boys to try the climb. Halfway up the overhang, he shouted that he was stuck, but before his friends could get to him, Ishmael lost his grip and fell to the ground. Jonathan remembered with great shame and sorrow how they'd had to carry his dead body back to his mother, but his friend's sad death had made him all the more determined to conquer the overhang.

He exercised for many days to strengthen his fingers, hands and arms, and then started the perilous climb, despite the desperate pleas from his friends not to try it. He was frightened, but knew he had to do this to overcome his terrors.

He was only just on to the overhang when his right hand lost its grip and he swung for a few desperate heartbeats until his left hand could hold him no longer and he fell to the ground. He took great care to remain upright and relax his body as much as he possibly could, landing on slightly bent knees to take the force from the drop and immediately going into a roll. He was completely unscathed, to the amazement and relief of his friends.

After a few more days of training, Jonathan was the first of his gang to conquer the overhang. It took him a long time and he lay on the top, shaking from the extreme effort of the climb, but he had strengthened his confidence and courage by doing so. He was also gaining huge respect from his friends for his achievements, especially as he had few natural talents. He wasn't an athlete, but made up for this by constant practice and determination. He was also smaller than most of his friends, but was very strong and fit with a good developing physique.

Little came easily to him academically, either; he learned subjects through hours of repetition. However, he had a natural talent for languages and the priests were amazed at how quickly he picked up new tongues and accents. He could speak most of the languages of his homeland, including those of the Israelites' enemies, and even if he didn't know all the words, he was an excellent mimic. He could imitate each one of the six Priests who taught him and his friends on a regular basis and one of his favourite pranks was to creep up behind his friends, then shout loudly in the same tone as an angry teacher, laughing raucously when they leapt into the air in surprise.

Jonathan had been born with a mop of curly brown hair, and as he grew, this mass grew, too. His friends laughed at the way his mane of hair bounced as he walked and ran, and they gave him the nickname of Lion Head, soon shortened to Lion as they learned to respect his tenacity and courage. They knew that they were the most important people in his life and he would always be loyal to them and protect them in difficult situations. They also appreciated his modesty; Jonathan would never talk about his achievements or lineage.

Chapter 3

Jonathan's Best Friends

Jonathan was a serious boy. Because of his burdens, he found it difficult to relax and enjoy life. Fortunately, his best friend Adam was a practical joker and a good foil to his more sombre nature.

Adam's father was a general in Saul's army. Adam himself was a tall and strong boy, and no one doubted that he would follow his father into a military career. He was also intelligent and a good listener, which was important for Jonathan when he felt the need to unravel all his thoughts and doubts.

A real treat for Adam and Jonathan was to visit Adam's grandfather, Manoah. The old man lived on the outskirts of the town and was rumoured to be ninety-three. Partially disabled, he would sit outside his house in the sun most days while teams of nurses came to look after him. The boys loved to listen to his tales, especially when he told them how he was terribly injured during a battle with the Philistines when they took the Ark.

"The Philistines were in a place called Aphek when we attacked them. We had thousands more men than they did, but there was a terrible slaughter. God was on their side that day and many of our men were killed.

"I was trying to guard the Ark when a huge man swung his axe and cut into the top of my head. I was left for dead. When my friends found me, I was barely alive and blood was pouring out of my head. I was cared for by our doctors for many days and there is no doubt they saved my life.

They had to fix my skull with staples and this operation had never been carried out successfully before. I am extremely grateful to them, and as a result of their skills and care, I have enjoyed many more years of life. Of course, I am not the same now as I was before the battle. I need nursing at all hours to keep me alive, but strangely, I developed a great skill with numbers almost straight after my encounter with the axe."

The boys were fascinated with his claim and gave him complicated mathematical challenges, which he always got right. They asked to see his wounds and he proudly showed them. His huge bald head had a massive, jagged scar right across the top where the doctors had roughly sewn the skin together over his stapled skull.

He also loved to brag that he'd actually known the famous Samson. "Yes, years ago, I met him near Philistia. He was one of the Judges of Israel covering the west of the country while Samuel was in charge of the east in these hills, but Samson originally came from here.

"Many of the stories about him have become enormously exaggerated over the years, but he was big, about twice the size of a normal man. And yes, he did kill a lion, but I don't think he did it with his bare hands; he was armed at the time. He also killed many of the enemy with the jawbone of an ass. Samson was a true eccentric. I don't think we will see his kind again."

"Did the Philistines really blind him?"

"Yes, they did – the cruel bastards. And he had a great weakness for women, which led to his downfall, but I don't believe that he became weak when his hair was cut. That's just too bizarre."

"Did he really knock down the Temple with his bare hands?"

"Well, I wasn't there, but yes, he did. He managed to budge two pillars, and this caused the roof to shift a bit. Once started, the damage just got worse until the whole building collapsed and hundreds of the enemy were killed. And, of course, he perished there as well."

There were many other stories told by this amazing man, and Adam and Jonathan never got tired of hearing them. In one, Samson tied torches to the tails of three hundred foxes and sent them through the fields of the Philistines, causing massive destruction. And then the devious Delilah brought about his eventual demise, getting her comeuppance when she perished in the Temple as well.

***

Another one of Jonathan's friends, Joseph, was the cleverest of the gang. He loved to invent and improve everyday objects and tools, and his friends had confidence that he would be successful every time.

Assuring Jonathan that he would design the best bow any soldier had ever had, Joseph spent days sticking long sinews and extra tendons to the convex part so that – he loved to tell people – it would have enough power to fire arrows from Gibeah to Geba. When Joseph had completed his adjustments, Jonathan suggested that they ride to the forest to try the bow out. The light was already fading as they raced off, with Jonathan comfortably in the lead.

Joseph spotted a huge buck on the edge of the forest.

"Look, Jonathan, there's a perfect target for you and a nice dinner for both our families."

Jonathan looked through the increasing gloom, saw the animal and drew back the powerful bow. It took all his strength, and then he released the arrow, which whistled past the surprised creature.

"Jonathan, you're supposed to point it at the buck first!"

Jonathan did not miss the second time: the arrow passed through the buck, killing it instantly. As they hoisted the animal onto one of the horses, Jonathan thanked Joseph.

"That's got to be the best and most powerful bow in the country. Even the legendary Samson would struggle to draw it. But I think you need to add strength to this part to give it more balance as it doesn't shoot straight."

"Nothing wrong with the bow," Joseph retorted, "but the shooter needs practice!"

After his success with the bow, Joseph told Jonathan that he would make him the deadliest sling in the whole of Israel. He made the strings longer and the cradle wider than any sling Jonathan had ever seen so that he could throw larger stones with more power and speed. He then gave it to Jonathan, who practised on a flock of birds flying past, bringing down two in rapid succession.

"Wow, this works even better than the bow!" Jonathan stated.

Joseph was watching his mother preparing the dinner one afternoon with fascination.

"Mother, why do you use that knife to trim the fruit and the vegetables? It looks really awkward and takes away much of the goodness."

"Well, that's the way it's always been done, over many generations. There's no other way."

This was a challenge to Joseph. After a couple of hours in his shed, he brought her a new implement.

"Try this on those cucumbers. Trim them using this side."

Trying the two sharp parallel blades, just a fraction apart, she noticed how easily and efficiently they worked. After thanking him for his clever invention, she couldn't resist telling all her friends how smart her son was. Soon all the local women were queuing for trimmers of their own.

Joseph also worked on improving the effectiveness of farm implements. He redesigned the scythe used to cut corn by observing closely how the current design was being used by farmers. His scythe was much easier to use, lighter, less tiring on the arms, and the new shape enabled them to cut at least a fifth more volume in a working day. Joseph's scythe was used for many centuries in his country, long after the inventor himself was gone and forgotten.

Joseph was short and a little tubby and disliked too much exercise outside. He was much happier in the workshop he had built in the family garden. He lived in Gibeah, the same town as Jonathan, and his parents were farm workers who looked after corn fields for local landowners. The family, including four children, lived in a small wooden house on the farm, leading a simple life. Of course, his parents were extremely pleased with the improved scythe, which made their lives much easier, although they often wondered where their son's intelligence had come from.

Despite his obvious talents, Joseph could be a difficult character with a huge ego. He could not adhere to time restraints and often insisted that a job would take as long as it took. If Jonathan asked him to work on a design, he would inhale a deep breath, expelling the air very slowly while shaking his head from side to side. Little annoyed Jonathan more than this reluctance on his friend's part to take action, but Joseph's inventions intrigued him so much, he had to bite his tongue.

Joseph was very interested in communications and spent many hours on improving the volume of noise amplified by rams' horns and trumpets. He worked out a system of short and long blasts to communicate any message, then developed a series of hand signals to back up the messages from the horns. He trained dogs to carry written messages to named people without deviating. Future communication methods, he believed, would include messages attached to the legs of birds, and he found that pigeons were the best for this purpose as they had the strongest homing instincts.

When Joseph showed off his latest invention, Jonathan wondered why on earth his friend was handing him two horns attached to a length of string.

"Take this horn and walk as far as you can over there and put the open part to your ear."

When the string was taut, Joseph spoke into the horn at his end, asking if Jonathan could hear him. Jonathan could, clearly.

"How on earth does that work?" he asked, bewildered.

"The voice vibrates the string very slightly and carries the sounds between the horns," Joseph explained. "I would like to be able to dispense with the string and vibrate the air instead. I'm working on it."

Every time Joseph met with his friends at the end of the day, he was fizzing with ideas which all came tumbling out of his mouth at once. While his friends shed tears of laughter at Joseph's enthusiasm, Jonathan evaluated his ideas carefully and adopted what he considered to be the best ones. Then they would all discuss amusing incidents that had occurred in the Temple. One in particular was remembered long into adulthood.

"Do you recall the day when I got into trouble over that cushion?" Adam would ask, and the friends would all chuckle at the memory. Ever the joker, Adam had laid a special cushion on the Priest's chair to try to liven up his dull lectures. As soon as the man sat down, all the boys heard a loud and indignant fart from the cushion. Unable to control themselves, they'd fallen about with laughter, but the Priest had been furious and demanded to know who the culprit was. When no one owned up, the Priest grew even angrier and said that they wouldn't be allowed to leave the Temple until the culprit came forward.

Eventually, Adam had put his hand up and admitted to being the guilty party, earning a well-deserved beating in front of the class.

"I still think Joseph should have shared in the punishment," Adam would say. "After all, he made that special cushion!"

Smiling smugly, Joseph would shrug away any suggestion that he was culpable, merely asking Adam, "Did the beating hurt?"

"No, I was expecting it, so I strapped another cushion on to my arse!"

Every time this story was retold, it brought forth uncontrolled hoots of laughter from Jonathan and his gang.

Chapter 4

A Lost Baby

I am Samuel, the High Priest, Prophet and Judge of Israel, the ultimate Ruler in my country. One of my most important responsibilities is to decide and appoint the King. My secondary area of responsibility is to act as the Arbiter in legal cases. I have my senior Priests in the Temple to assist me, but the final decision is always mine.

God spoke to me while I was still a boy and I knew from that day what I must do, what I was created to do. God had decided my destiny and my appointment was a huge privilege, but also a crushing burden. I have had to make many difficult decisions in my time, but the following story led me to make possibly the hardest judgement of them all.

A shepherd boy was in the hills of Qumran, near the village of En-Gedi, when he heard a noise that sounded like crying. Unable to find where it was coming from, he had difficulty identifying whether the noise was caused by a wild animal or a human. Eventually, after searching the area fully, he found a baby in a small cave. Wrapped in lace cloth, it had been abandoned, presumably by its mother.

The boy established that the baby was male and cleaned him as well as he could. He guessed the baby was only a few hours old, but there was no trace of his mother, or any other person in the area, so the boy put the baby into a bag and slung it around his shoulders. It was important to get the baby to a place of safety quickly where he could be fed with milk, and then rest after his ordeal.

The shepherd boy ran as fast as he could, carrying the baby to En-Gedi. Arriving after a few minutes, he called out for help. Two women who were drawing water from the well dropped their buckets and ran to him as he held the baby forward. He told them where he'd found him and they took the baby into a nearby house.

The baby boy was looked after by a family in the village for his first two years of life, and then the family approached the local Priest, saying that they could not afford to have another hungry mouth to feed. The Priest took the child, but was unable to look after him on his own. Eventually, the boy was taken to the Temple at Gibeah, where he was brought to me as the High Priest and Judge of Israel. I agreed that we would look after him and decided that he would be called Aaron, after the elder brother of Moses who was a Prophet and High Priest of the Israelites.

After a time, I became extremely fond of the boy. All the priests were delighted with him and took great pleasure in seeing him growing up, developing into a fine young man. I often wondered where Aaron had come from and made extensive enquiries, but as I did not have enough information to work on, I eventually gave up searching. It didn't really matter much as long as the boy was healthy and happy.

Then out of the blue, not just one mother turned up to claim him, but two!

I was in the Temple when a Priest came to tell me that a woman was waiting to see me, saying she was Aaron's mother.

"Bring her to me!" I ordered. She knelt before me and told me her story while I made sure Aaron was kept in another room.

"My name is Eve and I am from Jericho. I have a small business making dresses for the noble ladies in the City. Without warning, my husband ran off, leaving me heavily pregnant with our first child and little money.

"I gave birth to the sweetest baby boy and paid a man to take him across the border to the tribe of Reuben to find a family to look after him. The man, who was called Ephraim, came back to me and said he had found a good family from the Reubenites and I paid him the agreed amount. But I later became suspicious as he failed to give clear details of the family and their circumstances."

"Let me talk to my Priests in private," I said to her. "Leave us now, please, but stay locally so that we can talk to you again."

Then I asked one of my Priests to make some enquiries about Eve. He came back to the Temple a few days later and told me that there were rumours in Jericho that she was a prostitute and was ashamed because she had given birth out of wedlock. He couldn't confirm the rumours, but they left us uncertain about her version of the story.

I ordered Eve to come back to the Temple. "What did you do to find out the truth?" I asked her.

"I was determined to discover what really happened to my baby, so I paid a family friend, Matthew, to find out. He tracked down Ephraim and invited him out to a tavern and encouraged him to drink a flask of the best Philistia red wine to loosen his tongue. Matthew bought Ephraim a second flask as the sun was going down and asked him about his recent adventures out east, praising him for being a man of considerable courage and resourcefulness. He said he had heard that Ephraim had much experience with women that he was very interested to hear about.

"Matthew tried everything he could to get Ephraim to talk, and he succeeded to a certain extent, but the man spoke about anything except the baby. In fact, Matthew told me, he made every effort to avoid the subject.

"After several nights of this, Matthew grew bored with the boastfulness of his drinking partner and his reluctance to talk about what he had really done with the baby. During one of his many long ramblings, Ephraim bragged about how he had avoided paying thousands of shekels in taxes, and Matthew saw his chance.

"A couple of days later, at the start of the next drinking session, Matthew said he had a friend who was a local tax inspector, and he had a list of those he was chasing. Matthew said he would find out exactly who was on the list and how much he was looking for from each one.

"He reported back that Ephraim's name was on the list – near to the top! Matthew said he could have his name taken off the list, but he must have full details of all Ephraim's sources of income so that he could get his tax details deleted.

Matthew was amazed how easily Ephraim fell for this trick. It did not take long before Matthew got the full story about the baby and how much he had been paid. What Matthew did not tell Ephraim was that it was actually he who was the tax collector, and later he sent his men to Ephraim's house to collect their dues and lock him up in prison for his tax evasion crimes.

Matthew reported back to me that Ephraim had confessed to abandoning the baby in a cave and I remembered having heard the rumours about the boy who was staying with the Priests. That's when I came here to the Temple and asked to see him. And as soon as I laid eyes on him, I knew he was my son."

"There are many small boys here. Why are you certain this one is yours?"

"Well, he looks about the right age as I gave birth four years ago. I can't believe what a handsome boy he has become. I spoke to him, but of course he could not remember me; he just stared at me with his big doe-like eyes. I am certain that he is my boy, though, as I loved him immediately. But to make absolutely sure, I asked him to roll up the sleeve on his right arm, and at the top near his shoulder is a large birthmark. This proves to me beyond doubt that he is my son."

While I was deliberating over Eve's words, one of the Priests whispered in my ear that a second woman had arrived claiming to be the boy's mother. Rumour had it that she had also worked as a prostitute in the town and become pregnant.

I asked Eve to wait outside. This second 'mother', Ruth, was brought into the room and she knelt before me. I asked her to tell her story and why she believed that she was the mother of the boy.

"Well, sir, a few days after my baby was born, I woke up early in the morning and had a dreadful premonition that something was seriously wrong. My baby boy was lying next to me and was not breathing. He was very pale, and I was mortified that I might have smothered him in the night. Then people came and forcibly took him away from me.

"When I heard about the boy you have been looking after here, I became certain he was the one who had been stolen from me. I came here and have seen him, and I know he is mine. I have no doubt at all. I pleaded with your priests to give him to me."

I was in a deep dilemma. What should I do? I decided to dismiss her while I debated the case with my Priests. We talked for several hours, but were still no clearer as to the way forward.

I asked to be left alone while I prayed to God for guidance. Then I called for the Priests to come into the room, and bring the boy and the two women with them.

I opened the discussion. "I would like both of you to tell your stories again briefly and stake your claim for the boy in turn."

The stories had not changed significantly from the women's first accounts. It was time to take action.

"Bring me a sword," I said to one of my Priests. When he did so, I told him, "Lay the boy on the floor in front of me." I raised the sword above Aaron, feeling sorry for causing the poor boy such fear, but knowing there was no other way to solve the problem. Then I looked at the two women. "I am going to divide the boy in two so that each of you will have one half."

The first lady, Eve, screamed. "In that case, please give the boy to Ruth," she begged. "Keep him alive, do not kill him."

Ruth replied, "Yes, give him to me – he is mine."

I now knew the truth.

"Give the boy to Eve. She has just demonstrated that she is his mother."

Aaron went to live with his rightful mother, Eve, and she loves and cares for him to this day. She ensures that he comes to the temple daily for his education and training from us. I am so pleased to witness this, but we were all saddened to hear that Ruth was found hanging from a coat hook in her small house. Her mind had completely gone.

Aaron has shown amazing talent in all forms of art and is particularly skilled in wood carving. I allocated one of my Priests, a talented sculptor, to coach him and develop his extraordinary skills, and he has spent many hours teaching the boy how to use the various instruments to best advantage. I am immensely happy to watch him growing into a clever and brilliant young man.

I asked Aaron to make a model of our Temple, and although this task took him more than one year, the final result is quite magnificent. Then I suggested that he build a small model of the Ark of the Covenant and he readily agreed. The final work, which took him over two years, is no more than the length of a forearm, but is beautiful in its exquisite detail and is greatly admired by all of the priests. I am so proud of my protégé and count Aaron's achievements and development as one of the highlights of my life.

Jonathan is, of course, a regular visitor to my Temple, and he and Aaron have become good friends. I have a feeling this friendship will one day be of great benefit to all Israel.

Chapter 5

Jonathan's Other 'Friend'

In addition to Adam, Joseph and Aaron, there was a fifth member of Jonathan's gang. Mordecai was the eldest son of Barak, a merchant who originally came from the coast near Philistia and married an Israelite, Leah. Now living in Gibeah, they had four boys and a girl.

Barak used to travel many miles east of the country with a caravan of camels and horses to a city called Babylon, where he would buy rich cloth and gold and jewellery. He would also look out for new products and ideas, and had a good knack of finding items which would sell well in his own country. To get the buying prices down as low as possible, he had endless patience, spending days haggling. But he knew when to walk away. Often the seller would run after him, and then he knew he had won.

Another of his skills was to exaggerate the quality of his products. Only he dealt with valuable items which would get high prices back at home. This meant that he would often spend months away, but he became enormously wealthy as a result.

Even though Mordecai and his brothers and sister hardy ever saw their father, they lived in one of the largest houses in the area and had plenty of servants. The family also owned many fields and had dozens of workers producing crops and tending the animals.

It was with their friend Mordecai that Adam and Jonathan went out one afternoon to fish on the nearby lake. After an hour or so of inactivity, they moved further around the lake to search for more fertile parts, but with no success there either, they were about to give up and go home when a group of horsemen rode up to them. Ugly, wild-looking men with ragged clothes and big, mean knives hitched into their belts, their dark faces were scarred, and instead of teeth, their mouths were filled with black stumps. Their voices were rough, their accents strange.

They dismounted and grabbed the boys, tying them straddled over the backs of pack animals, then riding for hours towards the east. The boys were thirsty and exhausted when they were eventually untied and thrown to the ground. Two men kicked them towards a post planted by the fire where the three of them were trussed up and tied.

Being treated so roughly and cruelly, the boys were very afraid. For three days, they were only given a small amount of water and food. Dressed in their tunics, they were not given blankets, so when the fire died down, they were colder than they had ever been before. They were shivering so much that sleep was impossible. By contrast, in the daytime, they became badly burned by the sun, which they could not shelter from.

While they were waiting to find out their fate, the boys agreed that if questioned, they would say they came from ordinary families. They were certain that they had been kidnapped to be ransomed. Eventually, Adam was untied and taken to the large tent in the middle of the camp. The men repeatedly asked him who he was, but he was careful to avoid telling the truth and stuck to the story he'd agreed with his friends. If these men knew his father was a general in the army, they would demand a high price. One man took a hot stick out of the fire and kept touching it to the base of Adam's feet, causing him to scream in pain, but they were unable to force him to change his story.

His friends could hear his screams and their terror grew. When Adam was finally hauled back and retied, it was Jonathan's turn. He told a similar story to Adam's when questioned, as they'd agreed, despite also being tortured with the burning stick. At the time, Jonathan's father Saul had not yet been anointed King, but he was still the Army Commander, and it was essential that these men did not find this out.

Jonathan was eventually dragged back and retied, and then it was Mordecai's turn. Jonathan and Adam watched as he was pushed inside the tent, where they heard his crying interspersed with the deep voices of the men. But something was different. Something was not right.

When an hour or so had passed, Adam was becoming increasingly concerned. Then it struck him why.

"Don't you think it's a bit strange that we haven't heard any screams coming from the tent? We were much more vocal as the pain was awful."

"What do you think is going on in there?"

"I don't know. Let's not make a judgement before we have had the chance to ask him a few questions."

But Mordecai did not return. Several days passed and there was no sign of him. Despite asking the men repeatedly, the boys were none the wiser as to their friend's fate and they worried for his safety.

However, worrying wasn't their only pastime. These were boys of action.

One night, Adam whispered to Jonathan, "Look, I've managed to free one small strand of rope. Can you help me pull it loose?"

"Sorry, Adam, I am trussed up so tightly, I can't move at all."

Adam struggled to loosen the rest of his bonds, working at it all night. By the first light of dawn, his wrists were raw and bleeding from his enormous effort, but he was triumphant.

"I'm free, what a relief! I can't feel my arms and legs, though, as they are still numb, but if the coast is clear, I can free you when the pins and needles have passed."

He shook out his arms, tentatively getting to his feet and flexing his leg muscles, then he untied Jonathan as quickly as his stiff limbs would let him. When they heard one of the men returning, the boys, quickly wrapped the ropes around themselves and pretended to be asleep. The complacent man soon went away again without doing a thorough check, satisfied that the boys were still secure, and they immediately sprang up and ran towards the horses.

Hearing their movements, the guard, complacent no more, ran back to the tent to raise the alarm. In a moment, a dozen men were crawling out of the tent, moaning about the noise. The guard shouted and pointed towards the boys and horses, and they all set off in pursuit, shouting and swearing.

Managing to keep their panic at bay with a supreme effort of will, the boys scanned the horses, choosing one for its height and strong legs and shoulders to offer them the best chance of getting away. They leapt on, Adam taking the front position. Thinking quickly, he turned the horse's head towards the oncoming pursuers and crashed into their leader, knocking the angry man backwards into the dust. Adam urged the horse at speed through the pack, sending three more men flying from their mounts before they'd even had a chance to settle into the chase, and then galloping from the camp, not once glancing back to see how many men were following.

Adam steered the horse roughly in the direction they had come from. Even though he had been strapped across the back of the mule on their way to the camp, he had been careful to watch where they were going. The land was flat, but he could see the hills they would need to climb in the distance.

Looking back, he saw that his pursuers were about two hundred paces behind, and were slowly gaining on them. He urged his horse forward, leaning down to speak to him to encourage him to go faster.

***

But what had happened to Mordecai? What had been his fate?

In actual fact, and to his immense relief, the boy had been taken back to his village and left there with a message. He went straight to the Temple and told the priests what had happened. The news soon spread and the families of Jonathan and Adam rushed to the Temple to meet with Samuel and question Mordecai closely to get all the details of his ordeal and the welfare of the captured boys.

"The men have demanded payment of fifty gold coins by the end of the week, and then they will release each boy unharmed. If there is any delay, they will chop off their fingers. Each day you delay after that, they will cut off a limb." Mordecai then told the assembled company that the men had demanded he take the ransom to them so no one else would know where the camp was.

It was a terrible dilemma. The priests and families discussed how they could raise the massive ransom as it seemed to be the only option open to them. Where would they get fifty gold coins from, though? Mordecai's family could probably have afforded to pay the whole amount without much difficulty, but having got their own son back, Barak and Leah were reluctant to let him return to his captors.

In one of his saner moments, more frequent in those days before his mind went completely, Saul had a quiet word with Barak and asked him to give the two families enough gold to cover the ransom for the safe return of Jonathan and Adam. He promised Barak that he would be repaid in full afterwards, but Mordecai would have to carry the money to the men. Barak refused both requests.

In the Temple, Samuel prayed to God for guidance. Only God could help the boys now.

***

The gang of brutal men chased Adam and Jonathan relentlessly. The ground was rising now and the boys' horse was breathing hard as he climbed up the steep, rocky hill, but the going was even and he raced over it well. It was the same for the men behind them, though, who were gaining ground all the time, and Adam and Jonathan were becoming anxious.

Near the top of the slope, the horse stepped into a hole and tumbled, throwing the boys to the ground. They only just managed to avoid being crushed under the horse's body by rolling away. The horse was not so lucky; he did not move again.

The boys sprinted up the slope to their right with no idea of how to get away or defend themselves. Hauling their horses to a halt in a cloud of dust, the men watched the boys escaping. Then they dismounted and were only a few heartbeats behind the boys as they started to climb, but this time the boys had the advantage. Young and agile, they were faster and better climbers.

As they climbed higher, the air became misty and low clouds blew across the tops of the cliffs.

"If we can climb just a bit higher into the foggier part," Jonathan called to Adam, "we can hide from these men for as long as we want. I am sure we can lose them, and then we won't be far from home."

"I don't think I can go on much longer," Adam replied breathlessly. "I am so sore, hungry and thirsty, and I have never been so exhausted. You must feel the same as me. I just want to bury myself here and die."

"Well, we can bury ourselves for as long as we want as soon as we find a hole to hide in. In the meantime, we must keep going. Come on, Adam, we have nearly won."

This was possibly the first time Jonathan's leadership skills were put to the test, and they proved to be worthy. Many hours later, he and Adam climbed down the other side of the cliffs and made their weary way back home. Their families, and indeed the whole town, were overjoyed to see them back safely. God had answered Samuel's prayer.

Mordecai ran to welcome his friends back, hugging them. They responded warily, unsure as to whether he had betrayed them. Why had he been released while they had been tortured? Seeing the doubt in their faces, Mordecai protested his innocence, saying that the men had threatened to cut off his hands, and then kill him if he did not tell them the truth. Jonathan and Adam did not fully believe him, but they decided to give him the benefit of the doubt and accepted him back into their group.

Mordecai's family was not so leniently treated. Barak found himself ostracised by the community for not paying the ransom and doing more to support the boys. He had proved himself to be a greedy and selfish neighbour, and the people would never forget.

***

As time passed, the four boys, Adam, Joseph, Aaron and Jonathan, who was now better known as Lion, remained firm friends, working and playing together, as close as family members. And they stayed this close for the rest of their lives, Mordecai always on the periphery and never quite a part of the gang again.

But sadly for Jonathan, his idyllic childhood was about to come to an abrupt end. The time was coming for him to start his military training, and his father Saul was determined that Jonathan would become the best commander Israel had ever known.

Chapter 6

Training for Greatness

Saul appointed his Commander-in-chief, Abner, to be Jonathan's trainer, telling him to create the toughest physical schedule he could come up with. Jonathan was moved away from his beloved home to live in the local barracks with other soldiers. He had to rise early in the morning and run hard for an hour, observed and followed by a horseman. He was allowed a small breakfast of bread and fish, and then had an hour of hard sword fighting with three of Abner's best swordsmen. He suffered many cuts to his hands and body, but improved slowly until he was a match for the best of them.

After another short break, there was sling and bow practice. Jonathan started out firing at a stuffed dummy, and then moved on to fast-moving animals like rabbits on the ground and pigeons in the air. In the same way, he practised throwing a spear, first at inanimate objects, and then at moving targets.

The afternoons saw him fighting off his fellow trainers on horseback. Then he was taught how to wrestle, going up against some formidable opponents. In his first fight, his opponent grabbed and floored him, and Jonathan could not breathe as his face was forced into the ground. He was badly shaken, but as he had no serious injuries, he had to get up and go again.

Abner put him up against a hulking great creature with a big round bald head which blended into his massive shoulders and body. He was the biggest man Jonathan had ever seen, and to make matters worse, he had an evil grin. It was obvious that he was looking forward to making Jonathan suffer, and the boy tried hard not to show his fear.

In moments, the big man had him in the most painful grip around his neck that Jonathan had ever endured. He heard his neck muscles creaking, but there was nothing he could do to release the man's grip as the pain became unbearable. The referee must have called a stop to the fight, but Jonathan heard nothing; he was only aware that he'd been dropped onto the ground where he lay, shaking and crying. Feeling sick and dizzy, he had to fight against losing consciousness as he was carried out of the ring and treated by one of Abner's men.

Adam had been watching both fights and was horrified to witness the dreadful beating his friend was suffering. Jonathan had always been thankful for Adam's ability to listen and make sense of his worries, and the two young men talked long into the evening, with Adam advising Jonathan on how to survive this torment.

"Don't be afraid to fight dirty. You will not be able to defeat these monsters by fair means; they are much stronger than you, and don't forget they have been fighting and training every day of their lives. So, you will have to find other ways. Look for their weak points. It doesn't matter how big and tough they are, their eyes and groins, for example, are as vulnerable as anyone else's."

There was no respite for Jonathan. The following day, Abner put him up against two famous wrestlers, clearly expecting Jonathan to get a sound beating once again. As the first opponent, a giant of a man, walked towards him, Jonathan knew he did not have much chance – none at all if he fought fairly – so he swung his leg back and kicked the wrestler hard between the legs. The giant's head came down sharply towards the ground and, as he yelled in pain and grasped his groin, Jonathan chopped his hands down with double fists onto the back of his neck as hard as he could. The giant collapsed and Jonathan brought his knee up sharply into his face, breaking his nose.

The man's lungs emptied with an enormous roar, and then he fell silent.

He did not get up again.

Jonathan's next opponent was as wide as he was tall, his body resembling a huge circle. He was naked except for a loin cloth around his middle, his legs were like two short tree stumps and his inscrutable face had strange narrow eyes. Again, it was obvious Jonathan was up against a master. The man had been watching the previous fight, so it was unlikely Jonathan could use the same tactics.

As they faced each other and circled warily, Jonathan reached down and grabbed two handfuls of sand from the ground. In the same movement, he flung the sand into his opponent's eyes, temporarily blinding him. In confusion and pain, the man covered his eyes with his hands. He staggered as Jonathan stepped behind him, grasped his neck in a lock and pulled him backwards to the ground, his knee digging into the man's back.

With a grunt of pain, the man soon gave up.

Again, Adam was watching, and he later told his friend how glad he was that Jonathan had taken his advice. As well as relieved that he had survived. But there was no such support from Abner. He decided that Jonathan had learned enough about wrestling and it was time to teach him about battle strategy and tactics.

There had been around thirty major battles in the several hundred years since the Israelites' exodus from Egypt and entry into the Promised Land. The details of every battle had been carefully recorded, and Generals and Strategists continually analysed the success and failure factors and learned from their experiences. Abner commissioned a team of craftsmen to carve miniature soldiers and horses from wood and reproduced historic battle scenes in extraordinary detail. The old landscapes were created in stone and sand in an area around thirty paces square, and Abner used it to explain every hour of the battle to Jonathan before the next stage was designed.

At each stage, Abner explained exactly what had taken place, and then asked Jonathan what the Generals could have done better. He placed much emphasis on how battles could be won with fewer men and inferior equipment. Jonathan learned how to feint a retreat and an attack, and how to choose and use ground possession to his best advantage. He was trained how to deceive the enemy and gain, as Abner was fond of saying, an 'unfair advantage'; and then how to be utterly ruthless so that his enemies could never return to fight. He also learned how to cut off food and provision supplies from an army and deprive them of medical facilities, which could be just as effective a way to win a battle as fighting.

Of course, that tactic could be deployed against the Israelites as well as by them, so Jonathan was taught about the importance of always keeping his Army's lines of supply open. So many battles and wars were lost because men had no access to fresh weapons or clean water and food. Extreme tiredness was another major contributor to defeat, so Leaders had to ensure that their men had good rest whenever possible.

Over several months, they went through more than twenty battle scenes, and Jonathan had to work out the best strategy for each one. He learned how to communicate successfully with his Commanders, often over a large area, using voice, runners, horns, trumpets and arm movements. With the help of Abner and Joseph, he developed the inventor's new communication ideas using dogs and pigeons.

Jonathan was told in great detail how God had supported the Israelites and intervened using the forces of nature to help His country win, causing the sun and moon to stand still in the sky, sending earthquakes and hailstorms to kill their enemies. But nobody could explain to Jonathan why the Israelites also lost some battles, even though they had God on their side! In his own mind, he believed that they had won and lost battles through human endeavour alone, without any intervention from above.

Some days were spent on learning the political history of Jonathan's people and the skills of good governance. Saul brought in the most successful Leaders and Priests of his land to lecture his son, and Jonathan was given many documents to read at night. He was then closely questioned on the subject the following day. He was taught how to negotiate and win deals, and Saul sent his country's Ambassadors to teach him the skills of diplomacy and some of the richest men of the land to tutor him in economics and wealth creation. At the end of each day, there was a period for reflection so that Jonathan and his teachers could summarise the learning points from his successes and failures.

In the evenings, he had no time to relax. He was forced to run again or swim long distances across lakes. On occasions, he was blindfolded, taken by horse many miles from the barracks and dumped on the ground without food, water or weapons. He had to find his own way back by navigating by the sun or the stars. Before he was hunted by the Nubians, he was told he would be taking part in a chase to the death to put him under maximum pressure. At the end of the ordeal, when he had killed the lion, the last surviving Nubian half carried and half dragged him back towards the garrison. Jonathan was unconscious and had lost a lot of blood, and it took the Nubian two days to get him back to Abner. By this time, the Nubian was almost as ill and tired as Jonathan.

The Nubian, who was called Figel, told Abner how Jonathan had saved his life by attacking and killing the lion, and then related the whole story of how Jonathan had managed to evade capture and kill the rest of his pursuers. Figel asked if he could serve Jonathan in gratitude for saving his life. His request was granted, and Figel became Jonathan's manservant for the remainder of the young man's life.

Upon his return from the chase to the death and the battle with the lion, under Abner's instructions, Jonathan was carried to his mother's house and a team of doctors nurtured him back to full health. Samuel sent three Priests to assist and to pray for him. Jonathan had been close to death when he'd arrived back in Gibeah, and three months passed before he was well and fit enough to resume his training.

Jonathan had a lot of time to think while his damaged body and mind slowly recovered. He decided that he could not take any more of this punishment and bullying, and considered his options carefully. He could try to persuade Abner that he was not physically or mentally able enough for this treatment and ask him to intercede with Saul. But he knew that even if Abner agreed, Saul would never accept his request and would probably order more abuse. Alternatively, Jonathan could end his life. This would be so quick and easy; perhaps terribly painful for a short while, and then nothing. But he instinctively knew that this was not the way he wanted to solve his problems. He would not be afraid to carry it out, but it would be a cowardly act and he was not a coward. His life had a value and purpose, but as yet, he did not know what it was.

He could run away from the camp, but where would he go? If he fled from his responsibilities, he would not be safe in any part of his own lands, and it was foolhardy to think that he could go across to one of his enemies' territories. He would be captured, possibly killed, or held hostage, and if he were ever rescued, he would almost certainly be severely punished by Saul. He could form an alliance with the enemy, but that would be perceived as traitorous, and he was not prepared to risk that. Nothing could be worth that.

He decided to talk to his friend Adam and sent Figel to find him. Adam came at the end of the day and Jonathan blurted out all his fears and problems.

"I think you have done incredibly well so far; I doubt that anyone has survived such treatment before. Why don't you ask for a private meeting with Samuel and take his advice? I could set it up for you, if you wish."

As usual, Adam's counsel was wise.

***

Two days later, Adam took Jonathan to Gilgal, which was only an hour away on horseback. They travelled under the cover of darkness without telling anyone where they were going, hoping they would be back before they were missed.

Samuel hugged Jonathan and Adam and welcomed them into his house. Then Adam left the old and young man to talk in private. Samuel offered Jonathan a drink of wine, which he gratefully accepted.

"I heard about your dreadful ordeal and I hope that you are recovering well."

"Yes, I am, thank you," Jonathan replied. "But I was gravely injured, as you probably heard, and I feel very tired and drained after the past few months of constant training. I don't know if I can keep going at this pace. The work is relentless, and I am not sure what is being achieved by this constant abuse and strain on my body. I don't want to lose my life to it. What is all this for? What exactly is expected of me? What is my purpose in life? Am I to rule our country or not, and if so, do I have your blessing and support? I know you will give me good advice and I trust your guidance implicitly."

"Jonathan, you must have more faith. When I was a boy a little younger than you, I had similar questions about my purpose in life. Then I heard someone call me and I thought it was Eli, the Priest. When I went to him, he denied that he had called me. I heard the voice three times, and each time, Eli denied it was him. He told me to go back to my room and what to say the next time I heard the voice.

"'Speak, Lord,' I cried upon hearing the voice once more, 'for Your servant hears You.' And the Lord spoke to me. Since then, He has spoken to me often and answered my questions. He will do the same for you, if you ask Him. He may also call you as He did me. If you do as I do and take His word and trust in Him, all will come to pass as He tells you.

"You know that I am extremely disappointed with your father's behaviour and his disobedience to God, and I have vowed that neither he nor his line will rule over the Israelites for all time. I wish that he would stand down so I could choose another. Therefore, you are not destined to rule in his place, and neither will any of your descendants. I hope you are not too disappointed by this, but it is not your destiny to be King."

"No, I am not at all disappointed. In fact, I am quite relieved. I did not want the heavy burden of ruling my people, but I would have done the job if you had asked me to. So, what is my role in life?"

"As you know, you are undergoing intense training for the most senior role in the Army," the Priest replied. "As a new and emerging country, we are in the most desperate situation. We are fighting for our survival, for the freedom to live our lives and raise our families in peace, and we have been striving for this for hundreds of years. This is the land that was promised to us by God, but He will not secure it for us. Instead, He charges us to occupy the land and defend and protect ourselves from our enemies.

"He also charges us to obey His laws, which are etched upon the stones that Moses brought down from the Sinai Mountain. If we obey Him, He will help us in battle and in our struggle to survive and establish our nation.

"Ask God to tell you your purpose in life and the part you must play in your country's development. I will pray for you and your guidance. My belief is that your purpose is to become Commander of the Armies of the Israelites, but I also believe you have a role to support and assist the next Ruler, and this will be the most important role of your life. It is vital that you are successful and effective in this; if you are not, there will be terrible consequences for our nation."

Jonathan was pleased to have this clarity. "Of course, I will do everything I can to fulfil this role," he said, "even if it means I have to sacrifice my own life in the attempt. But who will this King be and how will I know that he or she is the Chosen One?"

"I will know who the Chosen One is as soon as I see him – or her – and you will come to know that I have chosen them through God. In the meantime, you must endure your training and learn to become the Commander we need to prevent our people from being slaughtered and wiped out forever."

As Jonathan left Samuel, Adam met him outside and wanted to know how the meeting had gone. Jonathan repeated all that Samuel had told him. As they mounted their horses, Adam wondered aloud if perhaps Samuel would have a word with Abner and ask him to modify his methods.

It wasn't long before Jonathan was fit and able to rejoin his camp and carry on with his training schedule. To his relief, he sensed a slight change in attitude from Abner and his men; maybe Adam had been right after all.

But further afield, the news was not so good. The problem with the Philistines was getting worse; they were slowly taking over the country, and Saul needed Jonathan's help and expertise urgently to support him, and perhaps even replace him if he was cut down. He also needed a battle partner to share the decision making and plan strategy, even though Saul tended to ignore any advice he was given. As a result, Jonathan's planned training programme had to be cut short by a few weeks.

Jonathan felt that his childhood had also been cut short and he'd had to grow up too quickly. There had been no time to develop his own character or opinions; he seemed to be permanently tied to long days of exercising and learning. Although much clearer about his mission in life after his conversation with Samuel, he yearned to have several months on his own to reflect and contemplate the issues that would face him in life.

But, of course, this was not possible.

Chapter 7

Love at First Sight

Jonathan was coming out of the Temple one day when he had the shock of his life. Walking too fast, he crashed into a figure wearing a long blue robe. Stepping back, he looked into the most beautiful face he had ever seen, calm dark brown eyes gazing at him with the deepest intensity. Mesmerised, he became lost in their depth.

The young woman had full cheeks, long brown hair – as he noticed when she took her shawl off and shook her head – and her skin had been coloured a golden brown by the sun. Then she smiled and he felt like he had been hit by a thunderbolt and lightning at the same time. He was dizzy enough to collapse.

He stared into her eyes a little too long, then coughed and muttered that he had not seen her before.

"My name is Naomi; I live with my parents on the west side of town." She spoke in the sweetest voice he had ever heard, and all of a sudden, he wanted to know everything about her.

"I study astronomy at the Temple under the instruction of a priest called Elijah, the country's leading expert on the map of the heavens. My father is an official in the government," she replied, smiling at his eager flood of questions. "He organises the annual census. My mother looks after our small vineyard at our home in Gibeah. And who are you?"

Jonathan replied a little shyly, and with some reluctance, "I am the son of the King and I am learning to support him in government and the defence of the kingdom. I hope one day to be appointed as one of my father's Generals and lead my own men."

"Then I am sure you know the man I have been promised in marriage to – Peter Absalom, who is a Senior Officer in your Army."

It was the most devastating news. Peter happened to be one of Jonathan's men and a good friend. He just could not believe his bad luck, although he was careful not to let his feelings show and merely told her he knew Peter well.

They talked for a little longer, and then they went their separate ways. But over the next few weeks, he found it very difficult to concentrate, his head was so full of thoughts of Naomi. He thought of her beauty and loveliness at every waking moment and wanted to ask her a hundred questions so that he could get to know her better. He thought of ways he could accidentally meet her again even though he knew that he shouldn't. A kind of madness had overcome him and he couldn't think about anything else.

His studies suffered and he got into serious trouble with his seniors. Gruelling exercise helped him to cope, but as soon as it was over, his thoughts and worries quickly filled his head again. Abner often became angry with him and once kicked him hard in frustration. Jonathan wondered if this madness was unique to him or if others suffered the same pain. He decided that no one else could go through anything so dreadful and yet as wonderful as this.

Finding out where Naomi lived, he took to waiting outside her house. If she came out, he thought, he could 'accidentally' bump into her again, but it was a futile exercise. Rather than engineering a beautiful meeting, he wasted many hours of valuable time.

They did, however, meet up twice purely by chance outside the same Temple and exchange a few words, but he was aware that it was not right for him to take things further. She was promised to another – his loyal friend. However, it wasn't easy to resist. Jonathan could not help but notice many more things about her: the sweet dimple in her chin; the way her dress swayed as she walked and turned; her acute intelligence; the way – in fact, everything about her delighted him.

"Did you know that your characteristics are linked to those of the constellation of Leo the lion?" she told him, referring to his birth sign. Naomi showed Jonathan how to identify the star formation that showed the crouching lion in the sky when the darkness came one evening. "You can see it up there. It is said that the first of Hercules's twelve labours was to slay the Nemean lion and the only way he could do this was to strangle it. His father Zeus then placed the lion in the sky."

Work and training commitments took over once again and Jonathan had no time to follow Naomi and engineer accidental meetings. Many months passed before he was able to go back into town again, but the pain and madness had not lessened one bit.

Then he saw her, in the market. On impulse, he bought a small bottle of expensive precious oil infused with flowers of the desert. As he walked towards her, she recognised him immediately. He spoke her name, and then offered her the bottle. Immediately, that lovely, warm smile made her face glow. She took the gift and they exchanged a few words. She asked if he had seen Peter. Yes, he trained with him every day, but Jonathan had never spoken to Peter about her.

They took a short walk together and she told him that after she and Peter were married, they would live in a wing of her parents' house. At that moment, Jonathan knew he could not see her again.

He went back to his training and tried to forget her, but it was impossible. Jonathan's mind was full of thoughts of Naomi: he had found someone he wanted to spend the rest of his life with, but she was promised to his friend Peter and he had no idea how to solve his dilemma. For the time being, he just had to get on with his life and mission.

**

Jonathan was having serious doubts about his beliefs and faith, despite his upbringing with Samuel and the Priests and their long hours of teachings. He tried very hard to believe, but he just couldn't and he was determined not to pretend to have faith in God just to appease others. His principles were too high for that.

He discussed his problems with Adam on the many occasions they met. Adam believed all he was told by the Priests, but he agreed that faith was a personal choice and they would respect each other's views. Regarding the Naomi situation, Adam was resolute that Jonathan should have nothing more to do with her. Indeed, he made Jonathan swear that he would not go near her again.

"Look, Lion, if you as much as look at her, I will come after you with a big stick. And I don't need to tell you where I will be jabbing you!"

Jonathan curtly nodded his acquiescence. He then changed the subject, telling Adam that he believed a nation had to create its own destiny. His people were almost surrounded by the Philistines and other enemies, and Jonathan did not believe there was a God to help the Israelites get rid of them; they had to have the courage and training to do this themselves. God didn't interfere in the ways of humans, so only the fittest would survive.

However, even though he did not believe that the Ark could change their fortunes, he knew that a symbol could be so powerful that the minds of men could be changed and influenced. Jonathan did believe that religion could be used in this way to control the men and promote good health and clean living amongst the people. Perhaps it helped to create loyalty and obedience, too, which were so important for their Army and developing nation, encouraging men to fight their enemies in the common cause, giving people laws, purpose and direction, and ultimately creating a settled nation.

Religion could also be used to control and influence their enemies, as had been clearly demonstrated by the power of the Ark. He concluded, however, that one's purpose was whatever a person themselves decided it would be. Adam agreed with this.

Jonathan did not dare tell anyone else about his beliefs, or lack thereof. Once, he had timidly and privately proffered some of his ideas to a junior Priest whom he hoped would sympathise with him. The Priest had been furious, and it had taken all Jonathan's powers of persuasion to stop him reporting him to his Elders.

"This is what puts me off about the Priests and God. I don't feel I can trust them now, except for Samuel, of course. He seems to be the only one I can speak to, but I would not like to get on the wrong side of him."

"No, neither would I. I once saw him hack an enemy King to death! He is no soft touch."

Recognising that religion helped to maintain the family unit, which was essential to underpin the structure of a country, Jonathan went on to state that there were many advantages to bringing people up in a religious environment. The symbols and ceremonies at the Temples had powerful influence, and the Priests arranged for the people to eat and drink together, strengthening the community spirit beyond the family. They all became bonded in a common cause, and as a result, there was hardly any crime or bad behaviour.

Religion had a huge beneficial effect on the arts: there were beautiful paintings in the Temples, magnificent books and writings, and moving poetry. All kinds of sculpture, pottery and metalwork had been created in the name of God. And, of course, the Temple buildings and religious houses themselves were examples of magnificent architecture.

However, having studied most of the battles in the Israelites' history, Jonathan believed that their outcomes had solely been influenced by the soldiers' skills and efforts, and all the claims of divine intervention were made up by the Priests and Prophets to convince the people that God was either pleased or displeased with them. He did not believe that God told the Priests to tell the people these stories, but that they came up with them themselves to frighten and control the people. That Joshua won a famous battle over the Amorites due to a fortuitous hailstone storm which almost destroyed the enemy was purely coincidence.

Adam agreed with some of this. "Yes, I think that God mostly gives us freewill to fight our own battles, but we must obey His laws."

God had never shown Himself to Jonathan, nor to anyone he knew. He retold the story about how God had spoken to Samuel to tell him his purpose in life, but God had never spoken to Jonathan. Why didn't the Priests and Elders have doubts like he did? Perhaps they did but were afraid to reveal them.

Adam and Jonathan often talked late into the night and developed their theories and ideas for the future, understanding their role in achieving and maintaining peace for their people. They also knew that they had a lifetime of duty ahead of them, and that it might be necessary to sacrifice their lives for their country.

They had enormous respect for and pride in Israel's Leaders, both past and present, recognising that they were all united in trying to defend their people from their enemies and looking for long-term peace and prosperity. The two men asked themselves when peace might be achieved and whether it would be in their lifetime.

Eventually, Jonathan and Adam felt comfortable in their own beliefs and determined to dedicate their lives to their people and country.

***

When the time came for Jonathan to form his War Council, unsurprisingly, it included his four gang members. Adam was Jonathan's Senior General, having proved his competence and courage many times fighting under Jonathan's leadership. One of his tasks was to train the men to such a high level that they would have the advantage over a larger force.

Joseph was already well-known in Palestine for his cleverness and creative mind. His job was to find innovative ways to deceive and defeat the enemy and improve the performance of the Army. Jonathan asked him to dream wild dreams of weapons of mass destruction, and then to help his developing nation to prosper and survive.

Aaron's job was the procurement of weapons and general supplies for the Army, and to keep and augment its funds and wealth. Mordecai was clever and resourceful, but still doubts remained over his trustworthiness, so he became one of Jonathan's junior officers. He was quite devious in his dealings and Jonathan hoped that this talent could be used in the Israelites' fight against the enemy.

The War Council planned their strategy and tactics to turn the tide of the war, to attack and beat the Philistines and push them back. Jonathan was the undisputed leader and the others trusted him completely. They knew he would always support them and their Army of one thousand men. He had the skills to fight and beat the Philistines, something his father had so far failed to do. It was amazing to think that he was still only eighteen years of age.

His first trial was not far away.

Chapter 8

Preparation for Battle

Jonathan watched the approaching Army from his high position. The midday sun beat down on the arid ground and the sweaty faces of the men indicated their discomfort in the intense heat. One had two vicious-looking scars on his face; whatever weapon had inflicted the one crossing his nose appeared to have taken the front of it clean off. His face was stitched up with wire, and Jonathan wondered who had caused this terrible injury.

Jonathan's attention was drawn by two men talking loudly in guttural accents. As he looked in their direction, he caught sight of a flash of long blond hair, tied back and plaited. The blond man stood out as all his comrades had jet black hair and dark features. Nearby, a giant stood two heads taller than everyone else. Although his rolls of fat wobbled as he walked, he gave the impression that he was massively strong.

These were fierce men, travelling through the pass to strengthen the garrison of Geba less than one mile beyond. Their scowling bearded faces, skin browned under a thousand sweltering suns, lank dark hair hanging down the sides of their heads, and general unwashed and unkempt appearance told of the harsh life they had endured.

They wore rough plain tunics which hung down to their knees, stained by carelessly spilt liquid from many nights' eating and drinking. Their waists were drawn in with knotted ropes. Their leather sandals were laced up to their knees and scuffed and worn from many marches. Some wore metal helmets secured with straps tied under their chins, and others had breastplates and random pieces of armour protecting other body parts. They carried vicious-looking swords, axes and spears, mostly tucked into their rope belts. Some carried bows, with quivers on their backs.

Jonathan guessed there were at least five thousand of them. In addition, there were hundreds of women and children, straggling at the back of the column. The women oversaw the pack mules and camels carrying all the items needed for their long campaign: tents, food, weapons, clothing, medicines, rope, tools and drink. As well as many hundreds of pitchers of water, without which the Army could not advance for even one day, there were gallons of wine, beer, and rough spirit.

Jonathan had heard the stories about the vast volumes of drink these men consumed with gusto in the evenings around their campfires. A prisoner who had managed to escape from them talked of week-long binges with plenty of raucous singing and fighting – the Philistines were well known for their love of brewing and wine making.

These men were fierce enemies of Israel. They had defeated Jonathan's people in many battles in recent times and threatened to drive the Israelites out of their lands. The enemy came from the flat land along the coast which was known as Philistia, dominating the area in their iron chariots. They lived in five cities, the largest being Gaza.

More recently, their Armies had moved inland to try to conquer the higher rocky ground which the Israelites currently inhabited, but fortunately, they could not use their fearsome chariots here to maximum effect. The Philistines wanted to establish trading posts so that they could buy and sell goods with people in the lands to the east. Jonathan knew very well that he and his people would be fighting for their survival against these vicious men.

The Philistines were known as the Sea People as it was rumoured that they had travelled across the ocean from Greece many years ago. They were industrious and self-sufficient in the provision of quality metals for farming and fighting. Experienced blacksmiths produced chariots and swords made of iron, giving the Philistines a strong advantage over the poorly equipped Israelites with their inferior bronze weapons. Jonathan determined that one day, his people would gain the technology and skills for metal working, even though his enemies were keen to keep the industry to themselves.

Jonathan shifted his position to stretch his limbs, which had been still for some minutes. He lay on top of the steep slope of the small valley, looking sideways at his men, and to those on the opposite side of the ravine who were waiting for his signal to strike. He then looked across at the remainder of his Army on the other side of the valley, all well concealed from the Philistines. He had about eight hundred men here, but they were well outnumbered by the enemy.

He was concerned. Some of his men were holding farm and household implements such as scythes and knives; others had swords and daggers, but these were made of inferior materials compared to those of the Philistines. However, Jonathan had a huge and heavy iron sword which his father had given him, and some of his senior officers had good quality weapons, too.

Jonathan was very proud of his sling men, or slingers. He had trained them personally, although many of them had been experts from a young age. Joseph had improved his earlier sling design; each one now had a leather pouch for a stone with two strings tied to each side, the strings being the length of an arm. One string had a loop at the end that a man would put around his middle finger, and the other had a knot tied at the end.

The slinger would select a round fist-sized stone from the ground. As he flung it, he would let go of the knot just at the top of the swing. With a lot of practice, this allowed the stone to be thrown further and faster with great force and accuracy. The sling became an extension to the man's arm and enabled him to throw stones further and faster.

Slings were very light to carry and cheap to produce, and the stones were readily available in most places. A skilful thrower could use just one overhead swing with a slight tilt off the vertical. Some swung the sling once or twice slowly to settle the stone. Whatever the throwing technique, it stretched and exercised every part of the body.

Even though the stones could not penetrate armour, enemies were often disorientated and agitated by them. When armour was missing, the stones killed men easily and, unlike with other weapons, the bodies were not mangled when hit. Sometimes, the stones were so deadly that they could pass through a body and severely hurt the man behind. Stones lobbed into the air would rain down on men's heads, and they could travel as far as a man could run in sixty heartbeats.

Slingers usually carried three or four slings as they were so light and small. These men had become an extremely important and effective regiment of Jonathan's Army.

Jonathan practised with his archers every morning. Joseph had designed a prototype bow of oak and instructed the archers on how to make their own. The wood was tough and flexible, and the men strengthened their bows with animal sinews, tendons and horns. Joseph said that the structure of the bow was similar to the make-up of a man: bones, skin, veins and blood.

They made their arrows with reeds using eagle or kite feathers for accuracy and guidance, and heads of flint. These arrows could be fired up to a distance of four hundred paces, although sometimes the bows were less effective in wet weather, and strong winds could blow the arrows off target. Carrying quivers on their backs to hold the arrows, the archers wore leather guards on their firing arms to save their skin being ripped off. The lucky ones would have shield bearers holding a small disc to protect their faces or longer shields to protect their bodies, but most had to rely on skill and agility to avoid injury.

And now, after all the years of preparation and harsh training, Jonathan wondered how his first taste of action would work out.

Chapter 9

The Battle of Geba

Jonathan raised his right arm to indicate to his men on the top of both sides of the ravine that battle should commence. The man next to him blew a blast on his horn, and this prompted one hundred men to do the same from the heights. The enemy soldiers whirled around. The combined blasts confused them and hurt their ears, and they raised their hands to cover them.

Ten slingers skidded halfway down the slopes on either side of the ravine and hurled their deadly ammunition into the enemy Army. The impact had horrible consequences; the slingers were using larger stones than usual to inflict the maximum damage and the speed of their descent to gain extra momentum, and they could not miss at this close range.

Jonathan heard the thwack of a stone hitting a man in the forehead. It felled him without him making a sound. Another man was hit on the helmet and fell to the ground, writhing in agony and confusion. He managed to get to his feet, but was very badly shaken and staggered around aimlessly. Other stones thumped into flesh, stomachs, ribs and thighs, and their effect could be measured from the screams and cries they produced.

Ten archers skidded down the sides of the ravine just behind the slingers and fired over their heads straight into the body of the enemy Army. Many Philistines were killed instantly. One arrow went into a man's eye, his screams of agony abruptly cut silent as it penetrated his brain. Meanwhile, the slingers had picked up their next missiles and were again hurling rocks into the masses.

This rhythm carried on for several minutes. The Philistine Leaders tried to rally their troops and shouted at them to charge the archers and slingers, but Jonathan's men had been instructed when threatened to climb back up to the top of the ravine where the enemy could not reach them and continue their onslaught from higher ground.

The first part of the battle had gone to plan; the enemy Army was seriously rattled, but Jonathan realised that their huge numbers, which he now estimated at more than ten thousand, would eventually prevail. He signalled to his trumpeters to sound the blast for the second stage of the battle to commence.

Around one hundred of his men attacked the rear of the enemy Army, avoiding the women and children in the baggage train who had retreated out of harm's way. The Israelites slashed with their various weapons, inflicting significant damage, but they were hopelessly outnumbered and were steadily beaten back by the Philistines. Jonathan was forced to watch as his men were butchered by the enemy's superior weapons: arms were sliced off and heads rolled, and the men who survived were suffering terribly from body cuts. This battle was turning into a slaughter and Jonathan was horrified to see more and more of his men being cut to pieces.

His Army was being pushed back. When Jonathan saw the extent of this devastation, he knew it was time to take alternative action..

Jonathan called to his trumpeters to blast the sound for retreat. At once, his men turned and ran upwards, climbing the steep sides of the ravine towards the overhanging rocks at the top of the slope. They had to leave their fallen comrades on the battlefield; there was no time to save them, so the wounded had to be sacrificed for the benefit of the rest of the Army. This was part of the strategy which had been agreed. Nevertheless, Jonathan knew his men would be mortified to know that not one of their friends would be spared.

Jonathan's War Council had spent many days planning this battle and had created a dangerous trap for the enemy. His men had worked for the last two weeks, carrying and often dragging many tons of rocks to the top of the ravine, preventing them from falling by securing them with ropes and logs fixed into the side of the hill. The trap was hidden by sheets of leather – hundreds of rocks, each one at least half the size of a man, suspended at the edge of the hill and disguised by tons of gravel.

Unsurprisingly, Joseph had been the mastermind behind this strategy and had been in charge of directing operations. And now, the enemy was being led towards the trap by the retreating Israelites, just as planned.

At the last moment, Jonathan's men skirted around the sides of the danger. The Philistines were moving upwards towards the retreating Israelites, many more men who had already walked through the pass running back to join them, seeing what looked like a unique opportunity to catch and slaughter their enemies.

At the next trumpet blast, coordinated by Joseph, the Israelites cut the holding ropes, and the leather above the overhang released the deadly rocks. They crashed down the hill towards the climbing enemy, causing terrible devastation. Dozens of men were felled and pushed down the hillside, while the rest of them turned and fled. It did not seem possible that any of them would survive this onslaught.

The stones and gravel that continued to crash down on to the enemy were followed by heavy logs. Jonathan could not believe the devastating effect of Joseph's construction and he watched as dozens of the enemy were knocked over, their bodies pushed down the hill. A huge cloud of dust covered the whole Army, leaving the men dazed and confused.

It took many minutes for the dust cloud to subside. Eventually, some of the enemy who had been lying still started to move and wipe the dust from their eyes. Others would never move again.

Joseph's trap had worked well. Jonathan knew that it had only killed a few of the enemy, but the psychological effect would be enormous. The enemy had been completely taken by surprise and demoralised; their fortunes had been reversed in an instant when they'd thought they had the Israelites trapped and beaten.

Jonathan's men were spurred on, tasting the possibility of a victory which would be their first over the Philistines for many years. They had renewed confidence in their Leader Jonathan who had inspired them to this great achievement.

The slingers and archers were still firing their deadly volleys at the main body of the Army in the valley. Wave after wave, they kept up a steady onslaught. However, some of the enemy had started to climb the hill again, and their Leaders screamed at the others to join them. In moments, thousands of the enemy were on the move, climbing to catch the retreating Israelites.

When the enemy reached the top of the slope, they were led towards the next trap which Joseph had designed. During the battle, Joseph was by Jonathan's side, yelling with glee whenever he saw his ideas come to fruition. He had found a huge bitumen pit covering an area of about two acres. The pit was very deep, and he'd instructed soldiers to plant swords, daggers and other sharp implements into the bitumen at its base, their blades pointing up to the sky. The pit was disguised with long pine logs and covered with leaves, branches, gravel and sand.

The land approaching the pit sloped down sharply and Jonathan's men were running towards it, accelerating as they got closer. At the last moment, they swerved to the left and right of the pit, knowing exactly where it was hidden. The chasing Philistine Army, however, ran forwards on to the trap. The front runners just about reached the far side before the weight of hundreds of men following caused the logs to snap and the structure to collapse, plunging them into the pit.

The piercing screams and cries were terrible to hear. Many enemy soldiers were wounded by the hidden weapons, others were killed instantly. Some were stuck in the bitumen, struggling in vain to free themselves. The momentum of the men who had been running behind took them unwittingly into the pit, too, where they joined the writhing mass.

Many Israelites ran behind the Philistine Army. Fighting like demons, they forced more Philistines towards the pit where they fell headlong on top of the trapped bodies. The mass of writhing humanity screamed in terror; it was a horrible sound to hear, even from the enemy. Some tried to climb out of the pit, but were held back by a combination of bitumen behind them and the sharp weapons of the Israelites in front. As the extra bodies fell on top of them, they all tumbled to the base of the pit, the pile growing taller until some Philistines were simply able to step out – straight into a slaughter by the Israelites.

The tail end of the enemy Army was pushed and harassed towards the pit. The Philistines turned to face the Israelites and fight back, and a terrible battle ensued. But the Israelites were fighting with greater energy and renewed hope, while the Philistines were demoralised by the terrible pounding they had endured. They had been outwitted by the Israelites and reduced to around a quarter of their original number.

The battle was nearly won. Jonathan watched as the struggling enemy started to retreat in disarray, throwing their weapons to the ground so that they could run faster as they raced back down the slope towards the path, trying to get to the safety of Geba. But the Israelite slingers and archers were waiting in the ravine and fired on them mercilessly. Jonathan had ordered his men to spare none.

The chasing and killing went on for another four hours until the Philistine Army had been completely wiped out. Then the baggage train was taken captive, the women, children and animals rounded up. None of them was hurt, except the few who tried to fight back.

Jonathan had won his first battle. His men cheered and whooped with delight, praising their leader for their incredible success and God for their good fortune. Jonathan ordered every man to arm himself with the superior weapons taken from the fallen enemy so that they could be fully prepared for their next encounter with the Philistines. After raiding the baggage train, the triumphant Israelites ate and drank to capacity. Then, following a short rest, the Army made its way towards Geba with the long baggage train in its centre.

***

Meanwhile, Adam had been heading a small group of fewer than one hundred men who were hiding under an overhang on the far side of the garrison of Geba to the west. The garrison was situated on a steep terraced hill and the men had been there overnight to await their chance to take Geba.

The Philistine soldiers in the garrison had seen the main attack and most of them had left the city by the east gate, running to the pass to join their comrades in the stampede and leaving only a small force of men behind to hold the garrison and guard the women, children, animals, and provisions. Adam watched as more soldiers followed their friends through the pass to chase the Israelites, realising too late that the tide had turned against them. Then the time was right.

Adam ordered his men to climb the terraces as quietly as possible, then wait beneath the walls for further instructions. He guessed they had not yet been spotted by the few Philistine soldiers left in the garrison, so he ordered his men to climb the walls.

Using ladders, the men were on the top of the wall overlooking the town within minutes. They lifted the ladders over and into the town, then at Adam's command, they descended and rushed at the defenders. The battle was short and bloody. The small number of survivors tried to surrender, but Adam had been ordered to take no prisoners. He secured the garrison quickly, and then waited for Jonathan and his Army. When the Israelites came, he threw open the gates of Geba to welcome them with great confidence.

Jonathan climbed the walls of Geba and addressed his men from the top.

"Today, you have won a magnificent victory against massive odds. You have made history; you and Israel have defeated the Armies of Philistia and saved your nation from being overrun. We must all thank our God for this victory. Now it's time for you to relax and celebrate your wonderful achievements. Enjoy the spoils of war: feast, drink and dance, and take enormous pride in yourselves."

And there certainly was a lot to celebrate: the Philistines had suffered a terrible defeat for the first time in Saul's reign and the confidence of the Israelites had soared. Every single man was rearmed with the superior weapons of the enemy: swords and daggers, and some had armour and helmets made of iron. They had also taken a stronghold in their precious lands from the enemy. The Philistine soldiers had all been killed, while Jonathan's Army had suffered ninety dead and several dozen injured.

Adam and Jonathan and their teams had been planning this battle and preparing the ground for several months, assuming rightly that the enemy force would come to strengthen the garrison. After the celebrations that followed the Israelites' historic victory, Jonathan called his Council together to review the battle, but first they held a memorial service for their dead while physicians and local women cared for the wounded in the sanatorium. Jonathan visited them there to boost their morale.

The battle had been an incredible success, and Joseph received particular praise for the ingenuity of his two traps. Adam, too, came in for praise as his battle had been a total success without the loss of a single Israelite life. The deaths of good Israelite men in the ravine were regrettable, but the survivors agreed that this sacrifice had been essential for their massive victory.

Jonathan and his War Council talked about the next skirmish and agreed that their long-term plan would be to rid their nation of the Philistines and force them back to the coastal areas. There were other enemies threatening them, but action against them would have to wait for another day.

Jonathan sent runners to Saul and Samuel to report the good news. Saul was delighted to hear of his son's major success and sent his trumpeters all over Israel to announce the great victory. However, he was jealous of Jonathan having succeeded where he himself had failed and he instructed his people to proclaim that it had been his – Saul's – victory. On pain of death, they were ordered not to mention Jonathan's name.

But the people of Israel knew the truth. There was great excitement all over the land as the Israelites finally started to believe there was a real chance of peace, and they celebrated Jonathan as the new hero of their country. To Saul's irritation, they were now even calling his son Prince and Leader.

Chapter 10

Visions of the Future

Shortly after the Battle of Geba, Jonathan almost lost his life. He had taken two men to survey the enemy positions, and as they climbed a steep hill, the sky grew darker and darker until it was black as night.

They climbed on with some difficulty, a shower of heavy rain making the going even harder as it developed into a fierce hailstorm. The intensity of the storm grew worse and the stones grew bigger and hammered onto the men's bodies; they could not believe the ferocity of the storm as they fell to the ground and covered their heads with their arms against the constant bombardment.

Jonathan was the only one of them protected by a metal helmet, but he felt the effects of extreme exposure and wondered if they could survive this onslaught. The hailstorm was not letting up; if anything, it was getting worse. He looked at his two companions who had both been knocked unconscious. Then a particularly large hail stone hit his helmet with tremendous force.

Jonathan felt the air becoming warm; the cold and storm had completely disappeared, and he wondered how this could possibly be. A bright light was shining above him, and to his shock, he seemed to rise towards it.

When he was high above the ground, he looked down at the three bodies lying motionless. Though he was confused and frightened, he managed to keep calm as he slowly moved over the land in bright sunshine. The terrain below him changed from barren rock and stones to beautifully cultivated green fields with all kinds of vegetables and cereals and many vineyards. He could see hundreds of manmade water channels and sprays of water irrigating the crops. Blue lakes were filled with people bathing, and he could hear their happy cries and laughter. This scene went on for miles and miles, and he loved it, feeling no fear.

He saw white houses scattered across the landscape, reflecting the bright sun. They did not look like normal houses; they were more substantial and much bigger, built using clever designs he had never seen before. The houses became more densely packed together until he could barely make out any open space between them, apart from long roads which stretched in every direction.

The buildings became larger and he saw huge golden domes and Temples, and massive brightly painted structures. People were walking in and out of the buildings and along the streets, huge crowds of them in colourful clothing. The noise of the hustle and bustle rose up to him; the scene was a happy one and he would have been quite content to stay there and watch it forever.

However, he started moving again, faster now, heading towards the south. The buildings disappeared, and in their place, he saw sun-scorched hills leading to a huge lake. The air became hot and oppressive.

Further to the south, flying at greater speed over desert sand dunes, waterless and bare, he saw thousands of his people working under cruel slave masters, hauling huge stones with long ropes, allowed no chance to stop and rest. They were his people, bonded in slavery by the Pharaoh in Egypt, and he was sad for them.

He watched as warring tribes fought each other in seemingly endless conflict. As he moved northwards again, he saw his people in chains, being led away by invaders. The land soon became empty of people and he wondered where they had gone. Would they ever come back? This too made him sad.

Through sweeping mists, he saw a great King, wild and fearsome, and he wondered if this man was a future Leader of his country. Then Jonathan saw himself, standing behind the King in obvious support. But who was this Leader and where had he come from?

He then saw the future Kings of Israel and noticed that he was not among them. Because his father had disobeyed Samuel and gone against God's wishes, the Priest had vowed to take the kingship away from Saul and his descendants. Jonathan knew this as Samuel himself had told him, and he was not concerned about being passed over for kingship. He was, however, anxious to be clear about his future role.

He saw battles, guessing they were clashes yet to come between his Army and the Philistines. But after a dozen or so encounters, the battles suddenly stopped. Did this mean that his role was to lead his country to overcome the Philistines, then pass the responsibility on to another, exactly as Samuel had said?

A huge Army was marching in perfect order, wearing a uniform of armour and carrying formidable swords and spears. It was the most disciplined Army Jonathan had ever seen. Along each side of the road, tall wooden crosses had been planted into the earth, and he saw to his horror that his people were tied and nailed to them, dead or dying. Their bodies were streaming with blood from cruel torture and beatings, and those who were still alive were crying in agony and despair. There were thousands of them.

He was relieved when this vision eventually faded, but it left him feeling deeply distressed.

From the west, he saw horseless chariots approaching, huge metal monsters driving in formation ten abreast with long tubes pointing forwards. These tubes were spouting fire, creating huge explosions and deafening noise. Massive Armies of men were running away from these terrible chariots, but even more terrifying were the metal birds flying high in the sky. These too were spitting fire on to the people below and dropping massive explosive parcels to the ground.

Jonathan saw many roads criss-crossing the country with hundreds of small metal boxes racing along them in every direction. Massive cities covered most of the land. He saw that his people had amassed great wealth, but a long and twisting wall had been built across his country. Why was it there? Was it to protect his people from enemies or wild animals? Either way, it saddened him to see his country divided.

Jonathan understood what he was seeing: a vision of a future in which his people would continue to struggle for thousands of years, always surrounded by enemies. He was sad to see that wars would continue, the conflict futile in its relentlessness. Was there no other way?

Jonathan was lifted higher. Travelling at speed across the land and the seas, he saw many struggles across many nations. He saw great clouds of smoke and fires covering entire countries. There was war and strife everywhere. Would this never cease? Would peace ever come to the world? It seemed that humankind would never learn that they could not achieve their ambitions with force alone; people would have to talk to each other to resolve their differences. Overall, the future was depressing.

He drifted higher and saw a huge lion's head above him, staring down with bright fierce eyes through a wild curly mane. Jonathan recalled his horrible experience in the desert when an appallingly powerful creature had so nearly killed him. He could smell the beast's rank breath and felt sickness building up in his stomach. He saw its massive leg and neck muscles and its irresistible, unstoppable power.

Why was this horrible image tormenting him and forcing him to recall that awful time? The lion had come to represent his courage, strength, determination, and purpose, the essential image of his life. It was no accident that he was known as Lion. The creature was his symbol, his star sign, his spiritual appellation. He was Leo. The Lion of Judah.

A vivid light shone behind the image, blinding him with a kaleidoscope of colours. The rainbow fused together to create new colours that only came in dreams, bathing him in secure and comforting warmth. He fell into a deep unconscious state, but was still acutely aware of the happenings around him. He felt loved; all his earthly memories and pains were fading as his spirit floated higher.

Loving arms embraced him and gathered his helpless spirit into the bosom of a maternal angel. He surrendered to the eternal comfort without resistance. But the vastness of the lion's head seemed to fill the sky and the heavens. Its roar resonated with rough hoarseness, and its plaintive groan was heard throughout eternity as if it were crying for humanity.

The light lifted the image higher and it drifted up towards the heavens to take its rightful place among the constellations. A huge eagle towered over the lion, flapping its powerful wings to show its majesty and superiority. It stood on a heavenly plinth which signified the permanency of its presence, gazing over the scene with authority. A gyrfalcon stood far to one side and observed with judgement, malice and disapproval.

There were many other spirit animals in this heavenly eternity, but none was as magnificent as the elephant with its massive grace and presence. It symbolised wealth and authority along with benevolence, reliability, confidence and great promise for the future. Millions of people would look up to and respect the elephant for its constancy and good judgement. It would reign supreme for many years and be revered for all time. Above all, the elephant remembered everything far beyond the ability of other creatures. But the elephant and all the other symbols would finally return to dust and only the Godhead would be left in eternal existence.

The Godhead was present, but invisible, causing the seasons to come and go in sequence and the grass to grow. It caused the thunder and lightning, expressing more power than any human could describe or imagine, creating the never-ending cycle of life and death; of birth and renewal; of the old and new; of rot and decay, growth and flourishment; of learning and ignorance; of seeds which turn into mighty oaks; of lofty mountains and fathomless oceans; of humans and animals. And the endless universe, which encircles the mere speck of dust that is the earth.

The Godhead created the space for love and hate, allowing its helpless and ridiculous humans freewill. In turn, humans have allowed the never-ending cycle of war, rape and destruction, torture and terror; the despoliation of women, children, animals and plants; the pollution of the earth's resources and the life-giving air; the terrible consequences of power and dictatorship; the mass annihilation of races, beliefs and cultures. And yet through all of this hell, hope emerges, love triumphs, and peace will come to the earth, at least for a short time. And the Godhead will again give mortal beings a chance to create heaven on earth.

***

Without warning, Jonathan plummeted towards the ground, crashing into his earthly body with a thump. His first feeling was disappointment that his vision had come to an abrupt end and he was once again being pelted by the frozen rain. He had found the experience enlightening, although in parts extremely depressing, but he had no idea who or what had caused it to happen. Was he a Prophet? He had heard them speak of similar experiences.

He had no time to dwell on it now; he had to deal with the harsh present and warm up his body. With great difficulty, he got his stiffened muscles working and rose to his feet, saddened to see that both his comrades had been killed by the pummelling they had received from the hailstones. He knew that he was lucky to have survived.

Chapter 11

The Hidden Passage

Another Philistine Army was massing at Michmash, a huge flat-topped mountain rising above an open plain about a mile away from Geba. It was rumoured that thirty thousand chariots were gathering there, and even though this was probably an exaggeration, it struck terror into the hearts of the Israelites, who had no defence against them and no chariots of their own. However, they were designed to travel the flat plains of the Philistines' coastal lands, while the Israelites were in the more mountainous eastern areas where the chariots were less effective. All the Israelites had to do was avoid frontal attacks by these deadly vehicles. A group of chariots charging at an Army of infantry men was a very uneven contest.

These vehicles, made of wood and iron, and pulled by two horses, were copies of Greek chariots which the Philistines had brought over with them when they first came to the coastal plains some hundred years before. They were driven by one man, with an archer strapped in alongside the driver. Sharp iron blades were tied near to the rim of the wheels, and any man in the chariot's path was either run down or cut to pieces, if he hadn't already been pierced by arrows.

The enemy also had six thousand horsemen and even more foot soldiers. The Philistines were clearly determined to avenge their defeat at Geba and wipe out the Israelites, taking over their lands. The Israelites had heard rumours that the enemy planned to set up trading stations to take their goods across the Jordan and beyond.

On three occasions, small bands of Philistines had left the camp at Michmash and raided nearby communities and farms. The need to deal with them was pressing. The enemy could not be ignored.

Despite Jonathan's success and the subsequent celebrations, many Israelite citizens and soldiers were fearful of this huge Army. Men who had deserted Saul's Army having lost confidence in his ability to overcome the enemy were hiding in caves, towns and villages to avoid the expected onslaught. Some were even saying that Jonathan had annoyed the Philistines too much, causing them to increase their forces to annihilate the Israelites. To make matters worse, Saul appeared to be more concerned by political arguments with

Samuel and taking the credit for Jonathan's successes than actually leading his people.

Samuel was furious with Saul, accusing him of disobeying God's orders and saying that as a result, his kingship could not continue. He had chosen another who would take Saul's place. As usual, Saul had lost his temper and stormed off to nearby Gilgal with many of his Army following. However, other soldiers and thousands of Israelite people were losing heart and joining the exodus. Some even crossed the Jordan to find sanctuary there.

During this time, Jonathan stayed in Geba, preparing his troops for the next campaign. Firstly, they needed to rest after their recent battle; they had been working hard for several months prior to their attack on the Philistines, but they all knew that the next campaign would be much tougher and more difficult. The enemy numbers were huge and they were encamped in a well-defended place. The Israelites' only option appeared to be a full-frontal attack on Michmash from the far side as the approach there was flat with easy access, but this would mean almost certain defeat.

Jonathan had several meetings with his Senior Officers, and with Saul's Commander in Chief

Abner and his Generals, but no one could suggest a workable solution. They looked at other ways to attack the Philistines, and even looked at their supply routes to see if they could starve them out, but in every place, they would have to face the deadly enemy chariots.

When Jonathan returned to Geba for more talks with his men, he was woken one night in his room at the garrison by Adam.

"We may have an idea how to launch an attack on the Philistines. There is a shepherd boy waiting outside who claims to know another way up to Michmash. If our soldiers climb to the top, we could surprise the enemy and at least inflict some damage on them."

"Bring the boy here."

Jonathan was up and dressed by the time the shepherd boy came in.

"What is your name?"

"Jesse, sir."

"Tell me about yourself."

"I look after my father's sheep by the wadi. There are about one hundred sheep and I protect them from ferocious wolves and other wild animals. I have never lost a sheep and would protect them with my life. I am twelve years old and come from Bethlehem, and I pass the long nights playing the lyre and singing."

"How do you protect your sheep?"

"I use my sling to frighten off the wolves and other wild animals, and if they persist, I deliberately hit them with the stones."

"What have you come to tell me?"

"There are thousands of Philistines on Michmash and they could drive all of us out of our lands. But I know a place where you can climb up to a small Philistine outpost near to the main Army, and you can get there from the main pass. It is not well-guarded. You need to pass between two large cliffs, one known as Bozez and the other Seneh, and you will find a place where you can easily climb up to the outpost, and then to the main Philistine Army."

"Have you been up there?"

"No, not all the way as I could not leave my sheep, but I have been far enough up to see that you can get to the top."

Jonathan called his War Council into his room at the garrison and held a short meeting. They talked and argued about the situation for an hour, one man saying that they should investigate this pass and report back. They could then take part of the Army up the pass and storm the camp.

Eventually, Jonathan convinced the group that he and Adam alone should climb the pass. "We can then decide what to do, but we must leave now before the dawn light exposes us. Do not tell anyone what we are doing and where we are going, least of all my father and Abner."

Joseph handed Adam a heavy shoulder bag. "Take this with you to the top. I have made some new weapons which you can use to defend yourselves." He took a small bottle from the bag. "I have made up twelve of these. See the cord which extends from the neck of the bottle and the liquid inside? Light the end of the cord with fire, and then count to three and throw the bottle towards the enemy. There will be a blast like a clap of thunder and fire will burn and spread over a large area. Be very careful how you handle this because although the liquid looks like water, it isn't, and it will fire up rapidly. Don't delay any longer than a count of three, or it will burn and kill you."

Jonathan wound up the meeting, reminding his team of his instructions.

"I do not want my father, King Saul, to know what we are doing or where we have gone. Otherwise, he will forbid us to go, lose his temper and threaten to kill me."

Jonathan and Adam took two camels, and then Jonathan called the shepherd boy over.

"Take me to this pass."

Jesse led them in the semi-darkness towards the wadi. As the path narrowed, they saw the cliffs. Jesse pointed out the huge rocks of Bozez and Seneh, and the narrow path between them.

"You can see that the cliffs each side of the pass are so smooth and steep, they are almost impossible to climb."

He led them through the small pass between the cliffs in total darkness. After a few minutes, the light returned and Jesse pointed upwards.

"Here to the left, an old water course has broken down the rock over many years and it's quite easy to climb."

Jonathan thanked Jesse, gave him a gold coin and asked him to tell no one about their encounter.

"Go back to your sheep. If any have been lost in the hours you have been away, I will replace them. Please tell your father this and explain that you have been helping me, without going into any details. Come back to see me in two days' time."

Jonathan and Adam spoke for a few minutes to assess the situation and plan their next moves. They tied the camels to a short tree and stepped over the boulders in their way. The start of the climb was easy; as Jesse had said, the water course had created a path for them, but it gradually grew steeper. They looked up towards where they thought the outpost would be, the half-moon casting a dim grey light to guide them. Jonathan pointed upwards towards a small plateau, but they couldn't yet see any signs of human life.

Adam was growing nervous. "What do we do now? It would be madness to go up there on our own. We could go back to fetch our men, but even then, we would be heavily outnumbered. What do you think?"

"There isn't time. We will go up on our own – that is, if you are with me."

"I think – rather, I know you must be mad to be considering this. It would be a suicidal move for us. There is little chance we can come out of this alive."

"Adam, we all know my father is quite mad, but I am pleased to report that, even though as his son, I must have inherited some of his traits, I have not been similarly afflicted. Well, not yet! I maintain that we at least go up to have a look."

"And I maintain that your judgement is wobbly and you are behaving as if you have been at the wine bottle. However, you know I will happily go up there with you as I trust your wobbly judgement."

Jonathan too suspected that this was likely to be a suicide mission, but he did not pass his fears on to Adam. The only other option was to face the Philistines from the plain, which was even more dangerous. This spying mission was the only way to find out the lie of the land and the position of their enemy up here; there was no time to fetch his men.

The light grew a little brighter, the half-moon emerging from the cloud cover and adding clarity. The air was still and cool. The conditions were good for them. They continued their climb slowly and nervously, peering upwards to get their first glimpse of their enemies as they guessed that the plateau would be well-guarded. The climb was still gentle; they had tackled much tougher cliffs before. This time, they could crawl up on all fours.

They had agreed that if the Philistines spotted them and came down to confront them, they would have to retreat as they could not possibly fight them while they were still climbing. If, however, the Philistines didn't notice them or decided to stay where they were above them, they would climb to the top and fight them on level ground. If they could capture the outpost, they could then bring their Army to the Philistines. Both men were well-armed with heavy iron swords and daggers, having selected the best available after their victory at Geba. Adam carried the bag given to him by Joseph on his shoulder. They also had their slings, but did not think they would be needed.

The light improved, and after a while, they could just about make out some misty figures at the top of the cliff. However, the dawn had not yet risen above the horizon. They climbed on.

When they reached the halfway point, they were spotted. The Philistines shouted to them in their guttural accents to stop skulking around, get out of their caves and come up and face them. They called all Israelite men cowards, claiming they behaved more like women. As plenty of other insults followed, the two made their decision. They continued their climb while the men shouted from the plateau.

It was now time to bring the fight to the enemy.

Chapter 12

The Fight Commences

Jonathan put his hand over a rock at the top of the climb and tried to pull himself on to the level ground. A man stamped on his hand with such force that Jonathan cursed and slipped back down towards Adam. Undeterred, he climbed up again and put his right hand on to the rock. The man tried to stamp on it a second time, but Jonathan was ready and pulled it away quickly. With his left hand, he swung his sword at the man's ankle. The Philistine leapt back in pain, giving Jonathan just enough time to clamber over the rock and stand before his enemies.

His first objective was to clear enough space to enable Adam to establish himself on top of the cliff. He swung his sword a few times and the Philistines stepped back. Jonathan had hoped that there would be no more than half a dozen men on this strip of land, which he estimated to be about half an acre in size, but he groaned when he saw at least twenty. He and Adam had little chance against that many.

He called out to Adam, who was already pulling himself on to the level ground. "Our only option is to attack confidently and aggressively. Are you ready?"

Adam stood firmly by his side, gently lowering Joseph's heavy bag to the ground.

"Yes, I am ready!"

Jonathan waved his sword at the enemy, screamed and ran forward. Three men faced him as he ran at them, and he swung his sword towards the one on the right, who tried to duck under it. The sword caught him on his left shoulder, and he screamed and fell.

That was one out of the fight.

The next man lunged towards Jonathan, who managed to step back just in time and the Philistine's sword missed his stomach by a hand's breadth. Adam swung his sword down and cut the man deeply on the neck, and he went down with an agonised yell. The third man tried to disable Jonathan by lunging for his leg, but Adam intervened and brought his sword down heavily on to the man's arm, almost severing it. Meanwhile, a fourth man had engaged Jonathan in a sword fight.

Clash after clash of sword against sword caused sparks to fly into the night air. Slowly, Jonathan forced his opponent back towards a small log fire. He pushed forward, avoiding the man's sword and locking his right leg around the back of the Philistine's knees, forcing him to fall backwards on to the campfire. He fell heavily. Jonathan stamped on the man's chest to push him into the red-hot embers and he roared in agony.

The dawn light was just starting to creep into the sky, illuminating the silhouettes around them. Jonathan turned around, greatly concerned to see that three men were attacking Adam. Their confidence clearly increasing at every step, they were pushing him back towards the edge of the cliff. Four men rushed towards Jonathan and he realised that he and Adam needed a miracle to survive this.

Just when all seemed hopeless, a crowd of men came down the hill from the nearby camp. In the dim light of dawn, they started to attack their own men, thinking they were an invading enemy. The men fighting Jonathan and Adam turned around in bewilderment and shouted at these unexpected attackers to stop, but panic had set in and the newcomers fought on as men terrified for their lives.

Adam dashed for Joseph's precious bag and grabbed it. Both Israelites ran towards some low rocks and hid behind them.

"Looks like God has intervened, again," Adam said sarcastically. The enemy carried on fighting each other, and Adam and Jonathan took the opportunity to climb up the curve of the hill unobserved. Reaching the top, they lay down and looked over to the vast Philistine camp in front of them, unable to believe what they were up against.

There were hundreds of large tents, baggage trains and a wooden pen holding thousands of horses. Hundreds, if not thousands of chariots were lined up beyond the pen. Jonathan guessed there were tens of thousands of men in the tents, but fortunately, most of them were currently fast asleep. However, others were running from the outpost into the camp, shouting and screaming as if they were insane, and the soldiers were awakening fast.

Adam and Jonathan spoke briefly, agreeing a plan of action. They ran down the short slope into the camp, Adam taking out one of Joseph's bottles from his bag and lobbing it into the first campfire they came to. Almost immediately, it flared up into a huge sheet of flame, and then exploded with a deafening boom. The two Israelites ran on towards the nearest tent and Adam stopped to take out another bottle. He lit the cord from the nearby campfire, counted to three and threw the bottle into the tent. The resultant explosion set light to the tent and the men within were trapped as they screamed in pain and terror. To add to the confusion, Jonathan called upon his linguistic skills, yelling in a guttural Philistine accent that the camp was surrounded by Israelites and they were being attacked from all sides.

Before long, men were running around in total confusion and the panic was spreading across the entire camp. More and more Philistines were rudely awakened from their slumber, rubbing their eyes in amazement and fear as their comrades shouted and screamed and ran around in panic.

Jonathan and Adam ran towards the horse pen and found the wooden entrance gate was roped up. Three men were guarding it, and though their eyes were wild with a mixture of terror and excitement, they were fully aware of their responsibilities and stood fast. Jonathan and Adam attacked them with their swords, killing the leading man instantly, and after little resistance, the other two were dispatched. But by then, more Philistines had noticed what was happening and were running towards them. Jonathan slashed with his sword at the ropes of the gate, and then he and Adam both hauled the gate open. The panicking horses charged out of the pen, knocking down the Philistines who had come to confront them.

Jonathan ran around to the back of the pen and Adam to a nearby campfire. Withdrawing another bottle from his bag, he lit the cord and threw it into the pen after a count of three. The mass of horses screamed in terror and rushed to get out of the enclosure, those at the back trampling over the bodies of their fellows in their desperation to escape the inferno. As more and more horses crushed up against them, the fences collapsed. The horses charged to all parts of the camp, knocking down men and trampling through tents. They crashed into the parked chariots, but while many were thrown over, the metal structure of the vehicles was firm, and hundreds of horses were killed or horribly injured.

The earth reverberated and thundered with this hellish chaos, the fires and explosions like a terrible lightning storm, illuminating the land as brightly as daylight. Men ran around in terror, trying to avoid the rampaging horses while believing that a huge Israelite force was attacking them. They were killing each other in their panic and the fighting increased as more men became involved. Soon, there was not one tent left standing. Fires flared up all over the camp and the air was filled with the shouts and screams of men, the whinnying of terrified horses and the booms of explosions. The sky was lit up with fires and heavy with smoke.

Adam and Jonathan looked at this scene in absolute amazement from the relative safety behind the pen.

"I just can't believe we created this chaos!" said Jonathan. "We couldn't have hoped for anything better."

"I wonder if there is any chance at all we can get out of here alive. But now, I really don't care, although I would love to tell the others about this."

"Let's go around to the far side of the camp to make sure the whole place is in chaos," Jonathan said breathlessly. "But be careful, we don't want to get into any trouble."

They crouched, crawled and crept around the camp, hiding where they could. When the opportunity arose, Adam lobbed more bottles into fires or lit them from the flames, throwing them into crowds of men and creating even more chaos as they exploded.

"I don't think we can do any more," said Jonathan eventually. "We have put the Philistine Army into confusion and now it's time to retreat. Come on, Adam, let's get out of here while our luck still holds."

Adam and Jonathan ducked down low and ran towards the outpost, dodging hysterical men and horses. This was an extremely dangerous environment, and more than once they had to kill to survive. As they were approaching the outpost, one huge man with a big bushy beard came running towards them, swinging his sword. Adam, who was nearest, swerved away as the sword came down like an axe, slicing into the skin of his thigh. He yelped in terrible pain and Jonathan charged forward, plunging his sword into the man's stomach. The giant fell back, screaming hoarsely, his body shaking as he hit the ground.

Jonathan took Adam's arm and looped it round his neck, helping him out of that terrible place. They walked down the slope until they came to the flat outpost they had first climbed to. There were now hundreds of men fighting each other and it seemed inevitable that they would be caught up in the melee.

Adam lit the last of Joseph's bottles from the campfire and threw it into the centre of the fighting men. The resultant explosion caused a big gap to open up and the two Israelites scrambled through it to the edge of the outpost, hurrying down the cliff to the safety of the wadi below. Although there were Philistines hurtling past them, they ignored Jonathan and Adam, only concerned with saving themselves.

As they reached the pass at the bottom of the climb, Jonathan stopped and tied his headband around the cut on Adam's leg to staunch the bleeding. He then helped Adam on to one of the camels, the two beasts frightened and frisky from the noise above. The men calmed them as they mounted for the short journey back, passing dozens more escaping Philistines on their return to the garrison.

They weren't to know that they were heading straight into an even more dangerous situation.

Chapter 13

Return from Battle

Saul heard the thunderous noises and saw the lights and fires on Michmash, and he sent scouts to find out what was happening. They reported back that the whole camp was in chaos and uproar, as if an earthquake had combined with a terrible storm, and the Philistines were killing each other while others were running away.

Saul called Abner and demanded a roll call of the men in both camps. It soon became apparent that Jonathan and Adam were missing, and he demanded to know where they were. No one could or would answer him.

Meanwhile, the Philistines were retreating from Michmash in greater numbers, crossing the plain where Saul had been planning his original attack. Saul called for the Priests to bring the Ark of the Covenant to him so that he could seek the way forward. He was told by the Priests to attack the retreating Philistines and slaughter them so that they could never threaten Israel again.

Saul ordered his Army to meet and destroy the enemy as they left the main route from Michmash and headed west. As Saul's soldiers moved forward, they were joined by allies, many of whom had previously hidden in caves having doubted that their King would ever win in battle. Thousands of Philistines were cut down.

**

Jonathan helped Adam into the camp when they returned and ordered doctors to attend to his wound. They agreed that the wound was not life-threatening, but Adam needed urgent treatment to save his leg. He was also suffering from weakness and nausea, but the doctors maintained that he would be back fighting in time.

Jonathan called for a meeting with the other members of his War Council and told them in detail about his and Adam's exploits at Michmash and the incredible outcome. He then asked for advice on the way forward. His Council agreed to support Saul to eliminate the retreating enemy, but advised Jonathan to keep out of his father's way.

"What the bloody Sodom was the liquid you put into those bottles?" Jonathan asked Joseph as the meeting ended. "They exploded with a terrible force and set up those fires with an unbelievable thundering."

"Well, I did warn you to be careful. I call the liquid God's bile, but I think it's best I don't tell you exactly how I made it. Let me just say that the source of the liquid was the bitumen pit we filled up with Philistines. It has enormous potential and I am going to spend most of my time experimenting with it. I believe that it could have great benefits for our people, but give me some time. I will report back to you in due course, Jonathan."

"Well, it has already had enormous benefits for our people as it has helped to destroy thousands of our enemies. I will be very interested in your findings, so let me know as soon as you can."

Jonathan and his men rode east and south to cut off the Philistines who were hoping to escape that way. Against medical advice, Adam rode ahead and led his Army of five hundred men to chase down the Philistines alongside Jonathan. They caught up with them almost immediately and the slaughter began. The Philistines put up no resistance; they were screaming and crying, still traumatised from their terrifying experience on Michmash and desperate to escape, and they had no fight left in them.

As he was riding alongside Jonathan, Adam felt faint and fell from his horse to the ground. Dismounting to help his friend, Jonathan also felt weak and recalled that they had not eaten since they left camp with the shepherd boy. He dipped the hilt of his dagger into the viscous liquid of a honeycomb by the side of the road and smeared it on to Adam's lips, and his friend sucked in its delicious sweetness, coming round almost immediately. Jonathan then took some honey for himself, allowing both men to carry on.

Mordecai, who was fighting with them, told Jonathan and Adam that Saul had forbidden any of the Army to stop to eat until all the Philistines had been caught and slaughtered. The King had said that this was the best opportunity the Israelites had ever had to rid the land of the pestilence of the Philistines and there was no time for anyone to stop.

"Anyone disobeying the King's orders," he said with a certain amount of relish, "will be killed."

Jonathan was astonished by his friend's words. "Surely my father does not expect us to starve to death. How can we catch these bloody unwashed without strength in our bones and muscles? Once refreshed, we can run them down with renewed vigour. Come on, men, help yourselves: kill some livestock and eat, and then we will follow these uncircumcised bastards to the ends of our beautiful land."

Hearing this, his men ran into a local farm, dragging out sheep and calves which they slaughtered for their meat. They lit fires to roast the meat, but their hunger was so great that they tore off strips of raw flesh and ate greedily. Then, refreshed, they continued their chase.

Hours later, Jonathan's tired soldiers made their way back to Geba. Saul and several of his men were waiting for them outside the main gates.

"I hear you disobeyed my orders," Saul roared at his son. "Because of this, thousands of the enemy have escaped. Now they will form yet another Army against us. No one disobeys the King, and so you will have to die. Seize them!"

"Yes, I am guilty," Jonathan replied angrily, "and if you're determined that means I deserve to die, then I will take my punishment."

Saul's men grabbed Jonathan, Adam and their team, tying their arms and legs and laying them in rows face down on the ground. As he was pushed to the ground, Jonathan's eyes locked with

Mordecai's; the other man was watching from the side lines, his face expressionless, but the fact he couldn't hold the gaze told Jonathan all he needed to know. Once again, doubts about Mordecai tormented his already troubled mind.

Saul called his axe men and lined them up, ready to decapitate his son and Jonathan's loyal soldiers. But his order was met by uproar.

"We are all guilty," cried one of the men who had followed Jonathan into battle, "and so you will have to kill us all."

"But remember this," shouted another. "Jonathan has saved us. Not only did we win our first battle against the Philistines under his command, but with Adam by his side, he delivered the whole enemy Army into our hands. King Saul, you may have killed thousands, but Jonathan has killed tens of thousands of enemy men."

"Either kill every one of us or none," added a third man. "The choice is yours."

His men then lay down alongside Jonathan, and soon there were several hundred of them on the ground. Saul knew he had been wrong-footed.

"We will cast a vote," he snarled at the crowd that had assembled. "Who wants Jonathan to die?"

No one moved.

"Who wants Jonathan spared?"

All hands went up. Humiliated and enraged, Saul turned and stalked away. Jonathan had more influence than he had realised and his own leadership was threatened. His passionate hatred for his son and his smug friends grew in intensity and he would not rest until he had exacted his revenge.

Saul wasn't the only one beating a hasty retreat; before Jonathan and his men were untied and allowed to go free, Mordecai had slunk off to save himself from the anger of his former friends. Later, the War Council – Mordecai conspicuous by his absence – met and talked late into the night about their experiences.

At the end of the meeting, Adam reminded Jonathan of their long talks about religion over the years.

"Perhaps you were wrong to dismiss God so quickly and maybe you should rethink your faith. How could we have defeated thousands of Philistines on our own without divine intervention?"

"It will remain a mystery, we will never know the full truth," Jonathan replied. "But I still believe it was a combination of our skill, Joseph's genius and a huge dose of luck..."

"And where did that luck come from? Who gave Joseph his genius, us our skill?"

Jonathan fell silent. He knew when he was beaten.

***

The news of Jonathan's success spread all over Israel and he was hailed and praised wherever he went. The story of how he and his senior officer had defeated tens of thousands of Philistines while they were securely encamped on their high mountain was on everyone's lips. At feasts and in the Temples, indeed at every gathering in the country, it was told and retold, and often exaggerated, the numbers of the enemy soon growing from tens to hundreds of thousands.

Samuel and the High Priests tried to convince the people that the victory was God's work; His intervention in the form of an earthquake and a terrible storm had brought about the Philistines' defeat, but nothing was going to distract the people from their adulation of Jonathan. When he travelled to Bethlehem, the entire population of the city rushed out of their houses just to get a glimpse of him. People wanted to touch him. Hundreds fell on to the ground in a frenzy of worship. Land workers, shepherds and farmers left their crops and animals and rushed to catch a glimpse of Israel's biggest celebrity. Women abandoned their chores and brought their children to him in hope of a blessing, or just to touch the hem of his clothing.

But as the crowds became hysterical, they threatened to trample Jonathan and his group to death. They were pushed towards the wall of a house, where the occupants reached down from high windows and screamed at Jonathan and his friends to raise their arms so that they could be pulled up to safety. There is no doubt these residents saved his life that day as a frenzied crowd of admirers almost succeeded where thousands of enemy soldiers had failed.

Similar scenes took place all over the land as hysteria gripped the nation. Everyone believed that God had blessed Jonathan and helped him to win this incredible battle. There were calls for him to be made King immediately, and some even thought he was the Son of God.

People loved to hear him talk and observe how he dressed and walked. His red headgear, known as a keffiyeh and made from a square cotton scarf, became the height of fashion, and a group of enterprising women started a new industry to supply the demand for 'Jonathan hats'. These women became some of the wealthiest in the land.

But Jonathan still had a job to do. He worked with the Priests to create a national government and write a constitution. He appointed his friend Aaron to head a team to bring wealth to the nation and strengthen the economy, which had been decimated by constant wars. Aaron crossed into other lands and took agricultural produce to sell. He then formed alliances with nearby countries, appointing Ambassadors to negotiate trading agreements and safe passages, resulting in tariff-free deals to allow trading on a level field.

An industrial revolution started in the Israelite nation, people making goods, from farming and kitchen implements to luxury bedding and furnishings, and all kinds of weapons. One of Jonathan's best decisions was to appoint Joseph as Design and Construction Minister to promote innovations in manufacturing and architecture. Possibly Joseph's most successful project was the packaging of minerals from the Salt Sea combined with plant extracts and oils to make beauty products for the wealthier women of the world. The demand was so high that despite increasing both production and prices every year, the Israelites could never make enough.

Before long, thousands of camels and donkeys were travelling to places as far afield as Egypt and Phoenicia, Syria and Babylon, sourcing goods needed by the Israelite people, including gold and silver. Aaron put his numerical talents to good use, making difficult decisions about trading rules and exchange rates.

As the wealth of the nation slowly increased, morale was high. Even Saul, his jealousy of Jonathan still simmering under the surface, left his son alone to get on with his work. But Saul's mental condition was worsening and his rages became notorious; he and Samuel continued to argue, and Samuel constantly regretted his decision to make Saul King.

Chapter 14

A New King in the Making

Jonathan watched as the boy staggered forward, dressed in armour which was far too heavy for him. After a few steps, he fell on to his front with a crash and lay still, his fall kicking up a small cloud of dust.

For a moment, there was complete silence. Then a ripple of laughter started with the men behind Jonathan and rose into an infectious crescendo, the men on the facing hill joining in. Before long, the hills on both sides of the valley echoed with roars of laughter.

Jonathan watched on with increasing alarm. He had seen the boy before at his father's court, strumming his lyre and calming Saul. The last thing Jonathan wanted was the wrath of Saul, always so close to the surface, so he felt a deep sense of sorrow at seeing the boy so utterly humiliated.

Jonathan ran down the hill towards the boy, reaching him in moments and unbuckling his leg armour.

***

Earlier, the giant had stood fewer than thirty paces away, bellowing his threats across to the many thousands of Israelites on the hillsides, and every man had been able to hear him. He was almost twice the height of anyone there and his body was massive with muscle and fat, his legs like tree trunks.

A bronze helmet covered his head and a coat of bronze chainmail protected his body, his arms and legs encased by separate metal coverings. A huge spear and a javelin were slung across his shoulders, and he was also armed with a sword and dagger. No one had ever seen such a monster before, and everyone was terrified.

"We have fought many battles in the past," he boomed. "This time, send a man to fight me. If he succeeds, then we Philistines will become your slaves. If I kill him, you will become our slaves. I challenge you to find such a man."

His voice bounced across both sides of the valley as the echo slowly faded.

Saul and his Army were afraid; not one of them had any chance against this man. The giant repeated his threats, but no one had come forward. No one except this young boy.

***

Jonathan helped the boy remove the rest of his armour.

"Thank you for this," the boy said. "When I told the King I was going to fight that brute of a man, he and his men laughed first of all, and then insisted that I wear this ridiculous armour. Can you please take off my breastplate? Thank you. I told them I couldn't even lift it, never mind wear it. Now off with my arm shields as well, please."

"That man is far too powerful for you. You should never have put yourself forward. I shall go in your place."

"No! I am, of course, very grateful to you for offering, but I must do this on my own. I believe that I can kill him and win the day for Israel. My name is David, by the way."

Several years had passed since the Philistines had been driven from Michmash, but hostilities continued between them and the Israelites.

"Please tell me, David, how are you going to kill this Philistine giant?"

"I have my sling with me, the one I use to protect my sheep. I'm a shepherd, you see? I often have to

158

frighten off or kill animals threatening them. Over time, I've become very accurate."

Jonathan was still worried. "That's all very well, but you can only kill him by hitting him on the head, and most of his head is protected by his metal helmet."

"There is a small area exposed on his forehead…"

"No one is that accurate with a sling! You are taking a terrible risk."

Jonathan guessed that the boy was only in his teens. David's face was tanned from working outside in all weathers and he was strongly built from all the exercise he took. He would soon grow into a good-looking and powerful young man, but at the moment, he was still a boy.

A boy with determination.

"I have faith in my abilities, and God. Samuel says I have been chosen by God to lead the people of Israel and protect them from their enemies."

Most people in his position would have been annoyed and jealous to hear this news, but Jonathan was simply amazed. He only cared about the protection of his people against their enemies. Was this boy really going to become the man

Samuel had told him about? It seemed a bit far-fetched. How could Samuel possibly know that a boy from nowhere would have the skills and ability to take on this enormous job and be successful? Surely this would be a huge risk for the Israelites. If David were totally unsuitable, the country could be destroyed in days. Jonathan did not believe that God had spoken, but that Samuel had made his own judgement – and his judgement had already turned out to be imperfect, as he had demonstrated with his appointment of Saul as King.

***

Saul's madness had worsened and his officers tried all they could to calm him down, but nothing seemed to work. Then one had heard David playing his lyre as he watched over his sheep and had been stunned by the beauty and passion of the music. He wondered if these lovely sounds could soothe Saul's fevered moods.

When Saul heard the music, he was immediately calmed. Lying down on his couch, he fell into a deep sleep. The medicine of the lyre had worked and Saul's officers and servants were very much relieved.

In fact, Saul became very fond of David and made the boy his armour bearer. As David accompanied him to many skirmishes and battles, Saul found him to be a strong and loyal supporter of great courage.

And so to this latest encounter against the Philistines. The two Armies were facing each other, the Philistines lined up along a high ridge and across the valley of Elah, and the Israelites along the opposite ridge, many thousands of warriors on both sides. Saul was leading the Israelite Army, but for once, David was not with him. At least, not to start with.

From time to time, David was allowed to return to Bethlehem to look after the sheep belonging to his father, Jesse. While he was there, God had told Samuel that the next King of Israel would come from the line of Jesse, and he and the High Priest travelled to Bethlehem to follow God's directions.

"None of these have been chosen," said Samuel in dismay after having been introduced to the many sons of Jesse. "But God is quite clear that the Chosen One will come from your line. Do you have any more sons?"

"Only my youngest, but he is a mere shepherd. He can't possibly be the Chosen One."

"Call him," Samuel replied, "and bring him into the house."

The moment David walked into the house, God spoke to Samuel and left him and the High Priest in no doubt. This 'mere shepherd boy' was indeed His Chosen One. Everyone in the room was amazed when Samuel anointed David with oil and proclaimed him the future King. Before returning with David to face the Philistines, Samuel asked everyone to keep quiet about this news. Saul would fly into a murderous rage if he found out, and not even David's skill with the lyre would be able to calm him.

***

Back in the valley, Jonathan felt huge empathy for the boy and determined to do what he could to help him, even though he very much doubted David's chances against the monster, whose name was Goliath. Jonathan held out his hand to help David to his feet. The boy thanked him and moved slowly towards the huge Philistine. A small stream was trickling a few paces away, and David reached down and chose three fist-sized stones which had been smoothed by the water over hundreds of years. He put them into the folds of his garment.

While David was preparing his sling, the giant roared. "Come closer, little boy, and I will divide your flesh between the birds of the air and the wild animals of the field."

"My God will help me to strike you down, and I will cut off your head and give your dead body to the birds and wild animals," David replied in a loud, clear voice. "You come at me with your spear, javelin and sword, but I come at you in the name of the Lord God who will save the Armies of Israel."

The giant seemed momentarily startled by the boy's confident statement. His eyes narrowed and he focused steadily on the approaching figure.

David was standing close to the giant; they were only about five paces apart, and the contrast between the two would have been comical if the situation had not been so serious and dangerous. David only came up to the giant's waist, and the two of them looked like a massive bull facing up to a small deer. The giant could easily have leaned over and struck David.

Jonathan watched as David put one stone into his pouch, settling it into position. He swung it three times before twisting and unwinding his body with enormous force, propelling the weapon forward.

Jonathan had never seen such a strong and skilful action before.

At the last moment, David released one string and the stone was projected towards the giant at such speed that it could not be seen by the eye. It struck the giant just above his nose and buried itself in the lower part of his forehead. The giant looked startled and staggered, and then his body seemed to freeze before he crashed forwards. He hit the ground with an incredible thump, causing reverberations which could be felt by Jonathan and some of the men near him, and heard by both of the warring sides.

David approached the body. Without hesitation, he drew the giant's sword from its sheath, lifted it and swung it down, cutting off Goliath's head. He picked the severed head up by its hair and turned to the Israelite Army, raising it high in triumph.

The soldiers who had been mocking now cheered, shouted and roared their approval at the death of their terrible opponent. Each man was secretly also very relieved that he had not had to be the one to face Goliath. David walked towards Jonathan, holding his prize, and together they climbed up the hill, making their way through the exhilarated men to take the bloody head to the King.

Saul was ecstatic with David's victory and immediately ordered his men to charge the Philistines. The Israelites raced down into the valley and up towards the Philistines who had already started to retreat. Many Philistines were slaughtered, their camp was attacked, and the Israelites robbed them of all their supplies. Those who survived ran for their lives towards the coastal plain they had come from.

This was a great day for Israel.

***

From that day, Jonathan and David forged a strong friendship with mutual trust and respect. They vowed to support and protect each other in all circumstances, particularly from Saul. In his madness, it didn't take long for the King to become openly jealous of David and he wanted to kill the boy. Jonathan had to intervene to save David's life many times as Saul tried again and again, but even so, Saul still got the opportunity to throw a javelin at David. However, Saul missed, and this failure caused him to descend into deep madness, crying and screaming all night and foaming at the mouth.

At almost thirty years older, Jonathan was like a father figure to David, and David looked up to him with great respect and affection. He admired Jonathan's courage and fighting ability, and over many years, he learnt a great deal from him.

David's success against the Philistines was unparalleled in the history of Israel, but he was a complex character. On the one hand, he was wild and fearsome, and his temper often flared, but paradoxically, he also played beautiful music with his lyre and other instruments, and wrote sublime poetry and psalms. David had great charisma and could hold a crowd of people spellbound using a wide range of vocal pitches and tones, moving them to passion and fervour. He would mesmerise them with his singing and poetry, playing the lyre so beautifully that tears would stream down their faces as they vowed to follow him into war or peace, violence or harmony.

There was no doubt in anyone's mind that he would become a powerful leader in their land. In the meantime, he was the most accomplished musician, singer and songwriter in all of Israel, and his following stretched beyond the nation to the neighbouring tribes and even enemies. Women in particular would follow in their hundreds wherever he went.

But many thought him to be a drunkard and a philanderer. He loved to follow a long night in the tavern with a tumble in bed with a whore. Jonathan could not remember how many times he'd had to send a team of loyal men to recover David's unconscious body and carry him back to his own bed. Indeed, the men fervently hoped he would be comatose, otherwise he could be aggressive and loud when they came to rescue him.

Unlike Jonathan, David had a strong belief in God and was certain that he had been specially chosen by Him. Jonathan had come to respect Samuel's judgement, but he wondered once again on what basis he had made the extraordinary decision to anoint David when he was only a child. How did he make these judgements and where did he get his information from? Jonathan could not believe that God had spoken to Samuel, especially as Samuel had made such a big mistake in Saul's appointment. Was God imperfect, or did He allow people freewill to make their own way? But if humans could decide their own destiny, this would mean that God would not be able to predict the future, so why did Samuel and the other Prophets try to see into a future that could only be unknown?

These and other questions filled Jonathan's head. He wanted to know what it was about David that Samuel had seen which had not been present in Jesse's other sons, and he was determined to speak to Samuel at the earliest opportunity to get some answers – that is, if Samuel was prepared to tell him.

Chapter 15

Jonathan's Marriage and Destiny

Eventually, Jonathan married his sweetheart Naomi and they lived very happily in her late parents' house. On the few occasions he took a break from military duties, Jonathan was at last content and settled.

The circumstances leading up to their marriage were not so happy, though. Peter, her first husband and Jonathan's dear friend and ally, had been killed when he was out with a small advance party to reconnoitre the position of the main Army of the Philistines. Sadly, they had been spotted by the enemy and Peter's party was ambushed as they came out of a pass. Thirty of the men, including Peter, were slaughtered, but a handful had run back the way they had come, managing to escape to report the massacre to Jonathan.

Jonathan was greatly saddened by this news and travelled to the spot where the dead men lay, identifying Peter's body. He decided to go immediately to Naomi's house and tell her the dreadful news. Naomi went into a long period of mourning after she had buried Peter's body in the garden alongside her parents and other family members.

But there was a devastating twist to this sorry tale. One man in Jonathan's Army believed that he had sent Peter on a suicide mission in order to steal his wife. This man reported his suspicions to the Priests, but after many weeks of investigation, the Priests concluded that the circumstances of Peter's death could not possibly have been foreseen and dropped all proceedings. Jonathan was greatly depressed about this accusation; he was completely loyal to all his men and would never have done anything so cowardly and despicable. All who knew him were angry that the case had ever been put forward.

All but one.

For a while, the accusation against him threatened to break Jonathan's heart. Adam was upset to see his dear friend brought so low and decided to investigate further. It was almost inevitable that his investigations would uncover the accuser as Mordecai. Furious, Adam went straight round to see Mordecai, who initially denied the accusation. But under interrogation from Adam, he finally admitted it. Adam hit him hard in the face and told him that if he saw him again, he would kill him immediately.

Mordecai's family had a connection to the Philistines: his father had originally come from Philistia. When he sought refuge with the sworn enemies of the Israelites, Mordecai was warmly received by the Commander, especially when he was able to relay details of the Israelites' military and political strategies, and Joseph's inventions. Eventually, Mordecai himself became a Military Commander with the Philistines; in the history of the Israelite nation, this was the biggest betrayal the people ever suffered. While Adam was pleased to have rid the nation of the traitor Mordecai, he could not have predicted the consequences of his action.

***

As Jonathan recovered from Mordecai's final betrayal and Naomi from her bereavement, he started to visit her at her family house. Gradually, they resurrected their friendship and love, and were married a year later by a Priest in Gibeah's Temple. Many members of Jonathan's family, including his mother Ahinoam, came to join in with the celebrations on the happy day. His father Saul, unsurprisingly, kept away.

Jonathan had come late to family life. Perhaps he had always been fated to be with Naomi and had kept himself busy with his military duties while she was unavailable to him. Their marriage initially produced no children; despite them both visiting doctors for consultations and opinions, all kinds of tests and various medicines, nothing worked. One doctor even insisted on drawing blood from each of them and mixing it together with powders to make a medicine, but this left them both feeling faint and Naomi no nearer to conceiving.

They consulted Priests and asked God for His help. They even spoke to a local woman who was known for her skills with magic and potions, but without success. Then Naomi made an appointment to meet with Samuel. After praying with her, he concluded that God did not want the couple to have children. He explained that God had a purpose which was not always evident to people, but His reason would eventually be revealed.

At this, Naomi gave up any hope of having children with Jonathan. But after five years of marriage, to their utter delight, she became pregnant. Unfortunately, she felt ill during the whole of her confinement and the doctors became concerned about her health. Then the birth was difficult as the baby would not turn in Naomi's womb and had to be pulled out with metal pincers. The boy survived the birth, but was weak and sickly, and his legs were damaged.

Sadly, Naomi did not survive the birth of her child, and with a very heavy heart, Jonathan buried her in the garden behind the vineyard, next to her first husband and family. He spent many months in deep mourning before his friends managed to persuade him to go back to his military duties.

Despite the loss of his wife, Jonathan was delighted with his sweet child and loved him dearly. He named the boy Mephibosheth after his wife's father, but tended to use the familiar version Mepi. Finding a good nurse named Rachel, he entrusted Mepi to her care and went back to his duties in the sure knowledge that Rachel would love Mepi almost as much as his own mother would have.

***

Saul was now over seventy years old and no longer took part in battles in the Israelites' seemingly endless war against their old enemies, the Philistines. Instead, he directed operations from higher ground. And it was from high on Mount Gilboa that he witnessed a horrible sight: his Army had fallen into a trap.

A group of several thousand Philistines were marching across a flat plain at the foot of the mountain. Jonathan, who was leading the Israelite Army, decided a full-frontal attack was the best option, believing that the Israelites would win easily, but a second Philistine Army was hidden behind the first and the Israelites were trapped in a pincer movement. They had no hope of survival. Saul watched helplessly as thousands of his men were slaughtered without mercy.

Runners came to Saul to confirm the inevitable news: Jonathan and two of his younger brothers were among the dead. Saul begged the runners to kill him and put him out of his misery. They refused, so Saul went into a nearby cave and placed the sharp end of his sword into his stomach, the handle wedged against the floor, and fell forwards. The sword cut through him and killed him instantly.

The Philistines recovered the bodies of Saul and Jonathan and carried them back to their nearby base at Beit She'an, hanging their bodies on the walls of the town. They could now destroy Israel, dominate the people and attack their strongholds, one of which was Gibeah. Mepi was five years old at this time and Rachel had to carry him from Jonathan's home before the enemy arrived.

Unfortunately, she dropped the boy as she was running over a hill on loose shale and Mepi broke one of his legs. She managed to get him to safety, but doctors said that this break, together with his previous disability, meant that Mepi would never walk again.

Some days later, David came to Mount Gilboa, the site of the terrible battle, and wept for the loss of Jonathan, Saul and his family. He cursed the mountain in deep sorrow and anger, declaring that Israel would go into mourning for a week. During this time, David wrote some beautiful poetry about their wonderful lives and their contribution to the life of the nation.

**

The Philistines were overrunning the nation of Israel and carrying out wholesale slaughter. David travelled southwards and set up his headquarters at Hebron, establishing a strong base there. To stabilise his position, David decided to conquer the small city of Jebus.

The Jebusites, a Canaanite tribe, were the original occupants of the land and the city was in a strategic position on a ridge which enabled a route north and south, and also provided good access to Jericho and the Salt Sea in the east. He sent his

General Joab to carry out this task, which had been deemed impossible, but David told him to access the fortress by climbing up a water shaft to hide his Army's approach. This he did, completely surprising the inhabitants of Jebus and winning the city.

Joab renamed the city Jerusalem, the City of David.

David brought the Ark of the Covenant to Jerusalem, helping to unify the twelve tribes of Israel, and he finally defeated the Philistines, forcing them back to their homeland on the coast. They never threatened the Israelites again.

King David ruled for forty years and changed the Israelites from a disparate group of people united only by religion into a full nation. Trading re-commenced with their neighbours and David built on the firm base which Jonathan had created in their land. He made new laws and rules and maintained a strong religious grounding. In turn, David's son Solomon continued to build on this solid foundation and increased the nation's wealth many times over, constructing a beautiful Temple to house the Ark in Jerusalem.

Jonathan's destiny had finally been revealed. Without his incredible courage and achievements, the nation of Israel would never have been formed. And without his protection and support for David, Israel's greatest King may have never come to the throne. For three thousand years, people have continued to view Jonathan's victory at Michmash as the greatest miracle of all.

"The beauty of Israel is slain upon thy high places

How are the mighty fallen!

Tell it not in Gath, publish it not in the streets of Askelon;

Lest the daughters of the Philistines rejoice,

Lest the daughters of the uncircumcised triumph.

Ye mountains of Gilboa

Let there be no dew, neither let there be rain, upon you,

Nor fields of offerings: for there the shield of the mighty is vilely cast away,

The shield of Saul, as though he had not been anointed with oil.

From the blood of the slain, from the fat of the mighty,

The bow of Jonathan turned not back,

And the sword of Saul returned not empty.

Saul and Jonathan were lovely and pleasant in their lives,

And in their death they were not divided:

They were swifter than eagles, they were stronger than lions.

Ye daughters of Israel, weep over Saul, who clothed you in scarlet, with other delights,

Who put on ornaments of gold upon your apparel.

How are the mighty fallen in the midst of the battle!

O Jonathan, thou wast slain in thine high places.

I am distressed for thee, my brother Jonathan:

Very pleasant hast thou been unto me:

Thy love to me was wonderful, passing the love of women.

How are the mighty fallen, and the weapons of war perished!"

David's lament at the death of Saul and Jonathan, 2 Samuel 1:19–27 Old Testament King James Version

Book two – Bert

Chapter 16

Salad Days

My name is Bert Sugarman and I am a Londoner. I was born on 30 May 1895, the day that WG Grace scored his 100th century playing for Gloucestershire against Somerset at Bristol. He was in his forty-seventh year and it was a bitterly cold day.

In May 1915, I went to war.

I had a conventional upbringing in London with my mum, dad and sister, growing up to be a big lad. By the age of fifteen, I was already just over six foot, and weighed fourteen stone like my dad. Although he wasn't as tall, he had a great big tummy, which suited him in his role as a chef.

I wasn't sporty, but I had plenty of friends to kick a ball about with, and I enjoyed watching football at Craven Cottage, the home of Fulham FC, and cricket at Lords. I worked hard at school and did reasonably well. My family lived in Fulham; there were four of us and it was a happy household. My mother looked after us and the small house lovingly while my father worked in the famous

Savoy and Claridge's hotels. He was a chef de partie and worked mainly as a saucier.

On rare times when my father had a day off, he used to read passages from the Bible aloud to us, and my sisters and I grew to love the beautiful and evocative stories. When we got to know them better, he would ask us questions. It didn't matter how often he read them to us and how well we knew them, we never got tired of these stories and we asked him to re-tell them over and over again.

When I was old enough to go to Sunday school, I already knew most of the Bible stories, but I still loved the lessons. I remember my first lesson with an old dear reading us the stories and I annoyed her by telling everyone the ending before she did.

We loved the Old Testament stories about Noah and the flood, the great battles, Daniel and the lions' den and Moses taking his people out of Egypt. How did it take them forty years to walk to the Promised Land? I'm sure we could have done it in a week or two, but it would have probably killed us!

We loved the New Testament as well and could visualise the Sea of Galilee and the disciples hauling in their nets; Jesus speaking to the five thousand on the hills above the lake and feeding them with five loaves and two fishes. How did he do this and all the other miracles? I very much hoped I could visit the Holy Land one day, but it seemed most unlikely.

Later at school, we learned about the Crusaders and their fight to win the Holy Land from the Saracens. They had terrible journeys across Europe which took months, and many died on the way, but those who survived built magnificent castles all over Palestine and beyond. I loved the stories about the adventures of King Richard the Lionheart and his arch enemy, the Saracen Sultan, Saladin. We all wanted to visit the country to see where all this really happened, but travel to those places just was not possible. There was no way we could afford much more than an annual trip to Brighton.

When I grew up, I understood that I would follow my father into the hotel industry. He got me a job as a commis chef in the Goring Hotel right behind Buckingham Palace. My father knew the Head Chef and put in a good word for me, telling me in no uncertain language that I must not let him down.

The hotel had only just opened in 1910 and was one of the newest and best in London. It was the first in the world to have all rooms with en suite bathrooms (one reporter queried the point of this and wondered if the hotel was expecting to have amphibious guests). I was so proud to work there and was determined to do my best and impress the Chef as we cooked magnificent luncheons and dinners in our restaurant and private rooms.

The owner, Otto Richard Goring, was a huge figure in more ways than one, and we were all terrified of him. To this day, his family still owns and runs the hotel. He was almost as important as the King; I only saw him once when I brought out the baron of beef, but on the whole, we all did our best to avoid him.

The Chef turned out to be a tough boss. We were terrified of him as well, but I greatly benefited from those early years working with him and learned so much. Today, much of the food is bought into commercial kitchens ready prepared, but not then. We had to learn basic butchery to get the maximum value from a carcass of lamb, beef or pork; we never wasted anything and made dishes to use every part of the animal. We spent days learning how to fillet all kinds of fish, too. Occasionally, we would get venison, and this was a great favourite amongst the regulars, as was pheasant and other game meats.

Our hotel was – and still is – famous for afternoon tea, and we had to keep up the good reputation. I became particularly skilled at crafting cakes and pastries, and I baked fresh bread every day.

I would get a bus from Fulham to Victoria to get to work, but if the sun was shining, it was lovely to walk the route. I had to leave home around 9am and would not get back until late at night, but we would get a few hours off in the afternoon. Some of us played snooker in a local club, others used to sleep in the staff room. Sometimes we would take girls out to a coffee shop or for a walk on sunny days along the nearby River Thames.

Due to the long hours I was working, I rarely got to see my beloved Fulham FC play at Craven Cottage. I still support them to this day, and my father was also a keen supporter. My best day out is also one of my earliest memories of when he took me to a game there and we watched the Varsity Boat Race on the same day from the riverside nearby.

In many ways, my formative years were idyllic, but when I was a young man, my world was about to change. War was coming.

Chapter 17

Off to War

At the start of the Great War, the Goring Hotel was taken over by the Chief of Allied Forces, General Pershing, and we all joined up. When I say we, I mean the whole kitchen brigade and half the hotel staff. A large group of us from various countries linked arms and sang our national songs as we walked round the corner to Victoria Station where the Army was recruiting. We were relaxed and happy, looking forward to our adventures. Meanwhile, the General had commandeered our kitchen where he had a direct telephone link to US President Wilson.

I didn't want to cook in the Army; I wanted to fight for my country. Fortunately, I had the opportunity to do so and I couldn't wait to get cracking. I was made Sergeant, shortly after I finished my training on the south coast, of a London machine gun group, a territorial. We were sent to the Western Front, and after eight miserable, muddy months, we sailed to a place I had never heard of before, Macedonia. We hated it there, too, so when we heard we were to be sent to Egypt and the Holy Land, we jumped for joy.

We became part of the Egyptian Expeditionary Force known as the EEF when we arrived there in 1917. This was allegedly the greatest Army in history in terms of size, equipment, quality and fighting power. There were around one hundred thousand of us and the same number of animals: horses, camels and mules.

We were fighting the Turks – Johnny Turk, as we called them – who we only knew from childhood picture books: big men with long, dark beards and baggy clothes. People said they were not fighters and would most likely run away if you said boo to them. How wrong they were: Johnny Turk was a brave and fierce fighter, well-disciplined with great stamina.

In our group, we were mostly good friends having been together for a couple of years, but unfortunately, several of our men had been killed or seriously wounded. As new men came to join us, we mourned the friends we had lost, and the new ones never seemed to be good enough to replace them. The atmosphere wasn't quite the same afterwards.

I recall the terrible hardships we suffered: the thirst and hunger and utter exhaustion; the constant deprivation; the pain of blisters and feet

cut to ribbons; the agony of sunburn and
sunstroke; the terrible loss of life of friends. The
limbs blown away and spilled guts on the earth.
The terrifying noise and explosions and the heavy
smoke, dust and choking sand. The carnage. Those
poor animals, thousands ripped to pieces. The
terrible gagging smell of rotting flesh and the utter
despair of shovelling sand on to a friend's corpse.

We spent many months in Egypt and Palestine,
experiencing the dramatic variance in the terrain.
The suffocating humidity of the Jordan valley, the
desperate dry heat of the Sinai and the deadly
Khamsins which almost killed us. The freezing
winter rains in the Judean hills around Jerusalem.
The cool green fields in the middle of the country,
creating carpets of flowers of many colours, but
utter misery for us. The sand flies and mosquitoes
nearly drove us berserk; we had almost no defence
against them. The scorpions terrified us and made
our lives hell.

Worst of all was the thirst. It is so easy for us at
home to turn on a tap and have more than enough
water to drink and bathe in. We just take it for
granted, but in sun-blistered Palestine, if we could
not find water every day, we would die.
Desperately thirsty men went mad and acted
totally out of character, crying like babies and

sometimes collapsing and dying. We were fighting for our lives – fighting for water. Even today, I get agitated when I see and hear a dripping tap.

And yet our mates thought we were getting a cushy number in a sideshow of the Great War, sunbathing by the sea, fanned by beautiful scantily dressed belly dancers, sightseeing in Cairo and Jerusalem. They envied us while they were constantly shelled in waterlogged French trenches or stuck at home doing dreary jobs. We were the forgotten soldiers in a harsh foreign land and our ordeal was later said to be the toughest of all the campaigns of the War in the biggest Allied base outside Britain and France. However, we were privileged to be in the land of the Bible, and the excitement of treading the same paths and breathing the same air as Moses, Abraham and Jesus, seeing the same sights and sitting on the same boulders, inspired us and drove us on.

When we were sent to Egypt from Macedonia, where we had been for more than six months, living conditions were hell on the extremely overcrowded ship. We were hit by a torpedo from a German U-boat, and while the strike was not fatal, the boat listed seriously to starboard and we were ordered to crowd down below to lower the centre of gravity so it could level out. The smells and deprivation we suffered down there were terrible; I don't mind admitting that I have never been more terrified in my life.

Protected by a couple of destroyers along with air cover, we were greatly relieved to be escorted safely to the port of Alexandria. Many of our friends had not been so lucky, their unprotected ships sunk by U-boats. We were given welcome leave when we arrived in Egypt and thousands of us headed for Cairo, but we were horrified by the state of the place: full of flies and filth and ragged people living in miserable slum dwellings. Many of the men enjoyed the alcohol, cocaine and hashish and, of course, the girls. Belly dancers were a revelation and there were hundreds of prostitutes whom men chased, so inevitably, the numbers of venereal disease incidences became huge. Afflicted men had to go to military hospitals in Malta where their recuperation took up to two months – and their pay was halved. Sensible men avoided the prostitutes like the plague – literally!

Of course, the officers enjoyed great luxury in Cairo. Our Major described his pleasure at sitting on the veranda of the Shepheard Hotel, sipping coffee and watching the thousands of people, carriages and limousines passing by. We lower-ranking men went in groups around Cairo and enjoyed seeing the pyramids and the sphinx. We couldn't have imagined how huge they would be from pictures in a book and we wondered how they could have been built by men.

When Field Marshal Allenby took over in 1917, he realised that the men were getting tired and needed breaks, so he created a kind of holiday camp by the sea in Egypt. Men could enjoy a few weeks of swimming and sunbathing and comfortable living under tents, which for many was a luxury. It was also an opportunity for us – I enjoyed one short break there – to get our clothes fumigated and washed. Some of us played sports in the water and football on the land and others raced horses, which started a betting frenzy. I mostly just enjoyed the rest and slept and ate well. What a difference this made to the men and our morale. We were much stronger to face the rigours of the campaign afterwards.

We came up through the Sinai Desert out of Egypt, riding in lorries through that dreadful place. Some bright spark had come up with the idea of laying chicken wire on the desert floor, and this enabled marching men and vehicles to travel across the sand with ease. When I say bright spark, I do not mean this in a derogatory way; if it was my choice, I would give him every bloody medal ever produced with a bar. Can you imagine if we'd had to march through a hundred and fifty miles of desert over loose sand? It was incredible to think that Moses guided the Children of Israel across this awful desert, and that Mary and Joseph took the young Jesus to Egypt for refuge from Herod, then went back again to Palestine. What a horrific and dangerous journey this must have been.

While we were there, our Royal Engineers started to lay the railway from Kantara in Egypt up to Palestine. They also did a fantastic job of laying a pipeline all the way across the terrible desert from the Nile and building huge earthworks for our Army. We were in awe of them and their skills and hard work.

We fought alongside many nationalities: Egyptian camel drivers, local Arabs, French, Italians and South Africans, and the exceptionally brave and resourceful men of the Australian Light Horse and New Zealand Mounted Rifles regiments. Later, thousands of Indians were sent to us: hard workers but often difficult to manage.

By the time we had arrived in Egypt, the campaign had been going on for a year or so. Johnny Turk had been forced up to Palestine and was now holed up in Gaza, but the appalling incompetence of our leaders had caused terrible loss of life and ground. On one occasion, our men had captured the important Samson's Ridge, and then they were ordered back. The same happened at Fort Ali Muntar – our men were again ordered back and to allow it to be recaptured, and then they were ordered to retake it! We all despised our useless leaders.

When Allenby was sent in, he got rid of most of the dead wood and the chinless wonders. Other commanders were 'bowler hatted', which was our slang for being ordered back to London. One was 'bowler hatted with a bar' as he was sacked twice! Allenby was greatly respected; he was feared by some, but there is no doubt in my mind that he changed the course of the War and finally won it for the Allies. He was gruff, tough and bold, and even though he drove us to hell and back, we all loved him. Morale improved no end. If anyone was trying to define what makes a good leader, he would be the perfect role model. He inspired confidence in us, and we just knew we were going to be all right and win this bloody war with him leading us.

Allenby moved his HQ from Cairo right up to the front line where he was within range of Johnny's big guns. He saw for himself exactly what was happening and inspected every part of our Army regularly, making it absolutely clear that our objective was the capture of the Holy City. We were incredibly excited and motivated by this possibility, believing we would succeed where Richard Coeur de Lion and his Crusaders and many others had failed. We were covering the ground of dozens of old battlefields recorded in the Bible, as well as those of the Syrians, Romans, Egyptians and Babylonians, which made us even more determined to achieve our objective.

We gave Allenby the nickname Bloody Bull, and the code to say he was on his way was BBL – Bloody Bull's loose. Once he intercepted a message when a signaller was waving it to the next unit and enquired what BBL meant. The quick-thinking signaller told him that there was a minor agricultural issue: a bull was on the loose. It's unlikely he believed this, but he said nothing.

We used to march to a simple ditty about Allenby, especially in the early morning before we became too tired and thirsty, and it put a spring into our step and cheered us up no end. I can't remember it all, but it went something like this:

"Send us beer and send us tucker,

Bloody Bull, ruddy...

Send us tea and send us sugar,

Bloody Bull, ruddy..."

There were at least twenty verses in the same vein. I know it won't make it into *Poems of the Great War* alongside Sassoon, Owen and Brooke, but it relieved the monotony and boosted our morale. It was a reflection of how much we trusted Allenby to deliver while he pushed us to limits we did not know we had, and then some more.

Allenby decided that he would not order a third attack on Gaza, but he convinced the enemy that he would. Instead, he directed his attack on Beersheba inland. Winning it, he outflanked the line of Turks back to Gaza. This was our first action in Palestine.

When we captured Beersheba from Johnny, we also captured the wells that Abraham had dug nearly four thousand years ago. Later on, we faced Johnny at Sheria. They fought like tigers to hold the place, protecting the well there – the single water supply for many miles and the only supply between there and Jerusalem. We had been marching for days with almost no water at all and we were in a terrible state. Our lips had swelled and burst, and flies were getting into the wounds, driving us almost suicidal. Some of us were temporarily blinded and we linked arms to help each other as anyone who fell would not be rescued.

We were desperate to win this battle as I am sure we would all have died from dehydration if we had not. Fortunately, we overcame Johnny and stopped him from destroying the well, but we still had to queue for up to four hours to get our first drink. To everyone's credit, we all waited patiently for our turn without pushing or fainting, even though we were four parts dead already.

This terrible experience taught us to be careful to ration our supplies and to make sure we always had some water. Indeed, we were trained to survive on a pint of water a day by slowly reducing our daily rations, and we trained our animals the same way to conserve our precious nectar.

We were now moving east towards the Judean hills, experiencing the beauty of the land of the Bible: the iconic shapes of the olive, palm, pine, cypress and the tall regal cedar tree; the beautiful flowers blooming soon after light rainfall, proudly displaying every colour of the rainbow; the rocks and stones sat upon by Moses and Joshua and Jesus as they witnessed the terrible history of this land; the smells of the spices, herbs and plants wafting in on the warm air; the dramatic rolling hills with their pretty bright white homes covering the crests; the deep wadis and valleys snaking away in all directions; the camels and donkeys who had stubbornly borne their masters through hundreds of generations over the harsh land. Their ancestors had carried Jesus's disciples and the Children of Israel away from their long captivity in Egypt.

To our incredible excitement, we were getting closer to Jerusalem and we began to feel that we were on a crusade to capture the Holy City. King Richard the Lionheart had crossed this land, and I could close my eyes and imagine him in full armour leading his men on. Sadly, he failed to capture Jerusalem. And now, we were here to free the people who had been shackled and exploited by a foreign power for almost four centuries.

Chapter 18

The God Squaddies

We were London boys having the most incredible adventure of our lives. Having been born in one of the largest and most magnificent cities in the world, we'd lived in small terraced houses and worked hard most of our lives, many of my companions as clerks and shop assistants. I was the only one in the hotel business. We'd rarely seen the sun and were relatively unfit and pale when we left home. The Great War was our big opportunity to change our lives dramatically.

We built ourselves up to an incredible level of strength and fitness and became brown as berries. Despite our dreadful deprivation, we were hardy and robust, although always hungry and thirsty. Our boots were worn out and our feet were blistered and bloody; our tummies were often poorly, every muscle ached, and our skin was bitten to bits by mosquitoes and sand flies. But we survived.

Our most precious possessions in Palestine were our Bibles and reading from them for an hour or so at night was our greatest pleasure. If we were not too tired and distressed, this helped to distract us from our deprivation. A group of six or seven of us, known by our mates as the God Squaddies, would sit around the fire, discussing the stories we had read. The next day, we would look out for the names of the places we passed through on our long trek and compete to find them in the Bible passages. It was surprising how many were mentioned.

I remember sitting on a ridge overlooking a large valley and a range of hills opposite. We would be here for a few weeks, and once we had fully rested and tended to our various wounds and discomforts, we soon grew bored. Then one of our group realised that this was the Valley of Elah where David had killed Goliath. To occupy the idle hours, we looked up the Bible passage which describes the event.

The Philistine Army had been encamped on the ridge where we were sitting, facing the Israelites on the opposite side. The ridges were a surprising distance apart, but we decided to climb down the terraces to the valley. We could imagine the scene: the atmosphere and the tension. In the middle of the valley, we came across a small stream and I reached down and picked some smooth round pebbles.

"Do you think this was the stream where David found the stones which killed Goliath?" I asked.

"It easily could be," replied Arty, who believed every word he read in the Bible. I tended to sit more on the fence.

"It's incredible that he killed him with the first stone," I said sceptically. "He must have been extremely accurate to have hit him first time, especially when he had such a small target area to aim at."

"It says in the Bible that Goliath was six cubits and a span. How big was he really?" asked Dave, another one of my friends who took the stories he read as literal descriptions of the past.

"Well, they reckoned that a cubit was the distance between your elbow and the end of your fingers, which is approximately sixteen inches, and a span is the distance between your outstretched little finger and thumb – around eight inches." I was the expert here! "I make that total about eight feet and eight inches: a really huge man. No wonder the Israelites were so terrified of him."

"I believe Saul felt threatened by David's friendship with Jonathan," said Harry.

"Well, I don't agree," Bill commented. He and Harry tended to be the cynics in our group, so it wasn't unusual for them to moot ideas that would lead to a healthy debate. "I think he disapproved of their friendship for other reasons. Look, David pretty much admitted that he felt a greater love for Jonathan than he did for women when he lamented the death of Jonathan and Saul. And Saul himself accused them of a romantic relationship. The Bible passage is very clear in Samuel 1, chapter 20, and Jonathan did not deny this."

"I think that passage is actually quite vague," said Harry. "Jonathan understood that his role was to protect David, the future King, and to make sure he got safely to the throne. He guided David in all things. Don't forget that Jonathan was as much as thirty years older than David, so he was more like a father figure to him."

"If Saul were around today, he would have been locked up in the loony bin and they would have thrown away the key."

"Either that or they would have put him in charge of the Western Front!"

"Or more likely the Charge of the Light Brigade."

And so the discussions went on. They were always very interesting and our debates were light-hearted. We were trying to relive the experiences as they were described in the Bible while looking at the evidence we could see – the geography, weather, plants, trees, animals, people and buildings in Palestine.

***

Occasionally, letters came through from home and I used to love reading the words Mother wrote about our family and the news in London. I could feel the warmth of our family home and see the familiar furniture and ornaments, the photographs in wooden frames, the precious china and the front room which were only used for visitors. The rest of the time, the front room was closed off and out of bounds so that Mother could keep it in pristine condition. In our more homely lounge, the log fire toasted our toes and kept us up late until we were brave enough to climb the draughty staircase and snuggle beneath the sheets in our freezing bedrooms.

My mother would write about Isabel, my elder sister, and how she was doing good work nursing the wounded in Le Havre. How I admired and looked up to her, and I really looked forward to the day when we could catch up on all our adventures. Our life experiences were so different now compared with those of our youth when we were always arguing and fighting about trivia. I also enjoyed hearing from Mother about all my favourite aunts and uncles and how their families were helping with the War effort.

We God Squaddies used to share our news from home when we had finished our Bible chats, reading aloud the letters from our loved ones. Some of the men had wives and children and I thought about how terrible it was for them to be separated from their families for so many years. It must have been awful.

I believe that hell really does exist on earth. There again, heaven also exists in so many ways: in our family lives, in our children and grandchildren, in our homes, in our work and achievements and in our faith. I always had my faith to look after me and I never lost it during all the horrors of the War years. Jesus promised that He would always take care of us, even beyond the grave.

***

The morning after our conversation about David and Goliath, Bill was up early, practising with a sling he had just made. We set up a row of empty tins and we all had a go, competing with each other, but a couple of us just could not get the knack of letting go of one of the strings at the vital moment. There were some near misses as stones flew in all directions.

After several hours of pinging stones at tins, Bill was the eventual winner. He was the only one who could knock down three tins with six shots, but this was typical of his competitive nature. Bill was an athlete who had taken part in the 1912 Olympics and competed in the 198-mile cycle race, coming fifth. His friend and fellow countryman Frederick Grubb had won silver.

Bill was tall and slim and kept himself fit. He was a good team member and was always eager to get involved. If I had one criticism of him, it would be that he had a short fuse, particularly when we were going through long boring spells with nothing to do. However, he really enjoyed our God Squaddies meetings and always fully immersed himself in the conversation.

"None of us has achieved the accuracy David demonstrated when he killed Goliath with his first stone," Bill said now, summarising our slingshot competition. "He had a very small target to aim at as a helmet covered most of Goliath's head.

However, he'd had many years of practice; he had been using a sling since he was not much more than a baby. We only tried it for one day."

***

As we moved west towards the Judean hills, the rains started, and that winter was to be one of the wettest in recent history. We were soaked during the day and soaked again at night; it was absolute misery to be wearing waterlogged uniform all day and be covered by sodden blankets when we tried to sleep. Our bivvy, which we propped up with rifles, was usually blown away by the high winds, leaving us exposed to the elements and totally frozen. Our friends in France would not believe that we were suffering in the desert as much as they were in the muddy trenches.

The animals suffered even more. They were already half starved, and the mud caused them to slip and slide – often down the side of a mountain. With heavy packs on their backs, they could not get up afterwards. Men often fell with them. It was pitiful to see camels skidding and sometimes doing the splits and we felt so sorry for them. They worked hard all day for us, suffering gunfire and noise, often only to be ripped apart by shells.

Our boots were wrecked and leaking, and clods of mud stuck to them, making walking a nightmare. It was ironic to think that a couple of months back, we would have been so thankful for this rain. Be careful what you wish for!

As we advanced towards the east through the Judean hills, we faced one of our toughest battles at Nebi Samwil, which was on top of a mountain just outside Jerusalem, the highest point in Palestine. This is where the Prophet Samuel was born and buried, and where he judged Israel for many years. We could see the whole of the magnificent Holy City from this high vantage point with its fabulous minarets and domes. That was one of the most special moments of my life.

At Nebi Samwil, Johnny attacked us three times, and each time, we beat him off. Our machine guns were firing almost non-stop as our position was constantly blasted by Turkish artillery, and the world-famous mosque on top of the hill was smashed to bits.

One member of our group, Herbert, was a casualty of this battle: a shell scored a direct hit and both of his legs were blown off, and he also received terrible injuries to his stomach. We considered putting a bullet into his brain to save him from any more terrible pain, but none of us had the courage to do that.

He looked at us with startled eyes as he was being taken away, the pain not having kicked in yet, and we told him we would come and see him soon. The stretcher bearers took him to Emmaus, a beautiful old monastery which the Allies were using as a temporary hospital, but he only survived a couple of hours. Unfortunately, we were not able to get to him before he died and could not hear his last requests.

I agreed with the others that I would visit his widow and children as soon as we got back home and give them his few possessions. The family lived in Elephant and Castle, and Herbert had worked as a porter at Smithfield Market.

The God Squaddies' meeting that evening was a very subdued affair; Herbert had been liked by everyone. He was the quietest and most modest member of the group, but we recognised him as probably the wisest and most caring of us all. He'd made sure that none of us had dropped out in our terrible thirsty march a few weeks ago, actually retracing his steps to lift Arty out of a ditch where he had fallen. Arty would not have got up again without Herbert's help. Then there were hundreds of occasions when a few positive and supportive words from him encouraged men to pick themselves up and carry on, often in the most appalling circumstances. His death hit us hard and reminded us of our own mortality and the loss of hundreds of our mates over the past couple of years.

Herbert had had a solid, unshakeable faith, and he was a good role model for all of us to follow. Our discussion that evening centred around the relevance of Herbert dying at Emmaus. This was where Jesus had appeared to his disciples after his crucifixion.

I read this powerful passage from Luke when Simeon, before he died, saw the baby Jesus. It somehow felt fitting and appropriate:

"Lord, now lettest thou thy servant depart in peace, according to thy word:

For mine eyes have seen thy salvation,

Which thou hast prepared before the face of all people."

Book of Common Prayer 1662

I read a further passage from Luke when two of the disciples saw Jesus here after his crucifixion:

"And, behold, two of them went that same day to a village called Emmaus, which was from Jerusalem about threescore furlongs

And they talked together of all these things which had happened

And it came to pass, that, while they communed together and reasoned, Jesus himself drew near, and went with them."

Luke 24:13, King James Bible

The path to Jerusalem was now open to us, and in our exhilaration, we walked on air to the Holy City, the home of our Faith.

Chapter 19

Jerusalem

We captured Jerusalem from the Turks, to the enormous relief and grateful thanks of its residents. The Turks fled east, but the fighting was by no means over. They tried several times to recapture Jerusalem, but were beaten back each time and suffered great losses, which weakened their Army considerably.

We were so proud to see Allenby walk through the Jaffa Gate into Jerusalem to accept the keys from the Mayor and we all cheered him. He was a great leader, and with his guidance, we had won through to the Holy City, overcoming so many horrendous obstacles. TE Lawrence was with him for this momentous occasion. We knew of his extraordinary exploits in the east and it was a privilege to see these two great men together.

We were thrilled to be in Jerusalem; we had dreamed of this day for nearly a year and had read all the Bible stories about this extraordinary city. Can you imagine us London boys in the Holy City which is the centre of our religion? Indeed, it is the centre of three world religions and the most important city of the Bible. It was a magical and mystical place for us.

We God Squaddies had a field day. We spent many days walking around, visiting all the holy places: the Church of the Holy Sepulchre with the Tomb of Jesus; the crucifixion site, Calvary; the Wailing Wall which had been part of Solomon's temple; the Garden of Gethsemane and the Mount of Olives, amongst many others. Somehow, despite our exhaustion and weakness, we walked with enthusiasm and renewed energy, striding upright with great pride.

Allenby had passed word down that Jerusalem and all its inhabitants and holy places should be treated with courtesy and respect. He was particularly concerned to get as much Arab support as he could. Of course, we agreed. He also asked every soldier to give up one day's pay to build a memorial to all the comrades we had lost in this campaign on the site where the surrender ceremony had taken place. Again, we all readily agreed. We would go on to be very proud of the beautiful monument, which still stands to this day.

At night, we would discuss and debate the genuineness of Jerusalem's holy places.

"Did you know that David was the real founder of this city and it was known as the City of David?" I said. "This was where Christ was killed by the Romans. I just cannot believe that we are walking in his footsteps."

Bill was argumentative as ever. "But I find it had to believe that the crucifixion site is right as the Bible clearly states that it happened outside the walls of the City."

"Yes, but it was outside the walls in those days," countered Arty. "Jerusalem has been attacked and destroyed so many times that its layout has been changed radically. Allenby is the thirty-fourth conqueror of this city over the last three thousand years."

Bill retorted. "I doubt whether any of these Jesus sites are real. They were chosen by Constantine's mother Helena in the year 325 AD, some three hundred years after the event. I would like to know how she chose them."

"They feel right to me, and I am happy with that. However, I think Jesus would have had something to say about all those bossy churchmen at the Holy Sepulchre and the cheap souvenirs and the money-grabbers."

"I don't think he would be saying – he would be doing. Remember how he overturned the tables of the money changers and sellers in the Temple? We haven't got very far in two thousand years."

"When you think that there is evidence of people in Palestine going back at least three hundred thousand years, we are talking about relatively recent events. Moses took the Children of Israel out of Egypt some three hundred years before the time of David, so then until now is about one per cent of man's time here. It puts it all in some kind of perspective."

Dave piped up, "I got a really powerful feeling walking through the Garden of Gethsemane and looking down to the Holy City. Those huge gnarled olive trees could have been the same ones that Jesus saw and touched. These trees can live for more than two thousand years."

The discussions went on for half the night over endless cups of tea. This was our relief, relaxation and entertainment after so many months of toil and suffering; we weren't naïve enough to think that our ordeal was over, and indeed, it wasn't. Some of our hardest times were ahead of us.

The next stage of our War was to attack Jericho, which was a few miles to the east of Jerusalem.

We were looking forward to seeing this place as all of us knew the story of Joshua's extraordinary victory when his men encircled the walls every day for six days, and on the seventh, a blast from his ram's horn caused the walls to collapse. There would be plenty of mystery there for much more debate, but we had many obstacles to overcome before we reached this ancient city.

Chapter 20

Arrival at Michmash

Johnny Turk had dug himself in on the rugged chain of hills just north of Jerusalem to stop us reaching Jericho. Near a small village high up on a rocky hill called Mukhmas, a division of Johnny's Army was encamped, and it was going to be really difficult to shift them from there. There was a deep valley between us and the enemy, and the chinless wonders had decided on a full-frontal attack from the other side where there was a relatively flat approach. Even though we were promised full artillery cover, any one of us could foresee that many of our men would be killed or wounded in this effort.

We were ordered to rest and had a few days in the camp with nothing much to do. This created the best conditions for a God Squaddies meeting: mugs of hot, steaming tea while we passed long hours in the evening around the camp fire, seeking biblical references for this area. Arty said that the name Mukhmas was familiar and he was certain that he had come across it in the Bible. This was a challenge and we all set about searching different chapters of the Old Testament. After about an hour, when none of us had found the reference, Bill suggested we should ask the Major if he had any ideas.

Major Vivian Gilbert was a great favourite amongst the men and many of us used to go to him with problems about family and other issues. He often advised us how to reply to letters from our loved ones, and gave us thoughtful and caring answers. He had been an actor before the War and had played in the West End and on Broadway. We knew that he took great pleasure in reading his Bible and he occasionally joined in on our group discussions.

He had been with us since our dreadful time in France and we had mourned together the loss of friends and witnessed their terrible injuries. He, like us, had suffered terrible thirst, hunger, desperate tiredness and dreadful deprivation. We all stank from months without a proper bath in this hot, sweaty land. We were all bitten – the insects and flies were no discriminators – so it was sometimes hard to remember that he was a senior officer. In truth, he was too nice to be an officer; he was more like a father figure and so grateful for every task we carried out for him.

We called at his tent and he was pleased to see us. Yes, he said, he definitely remembered reading about Mukhmas in the Bible, and he would get back to us with his findings.

In just a few minutes, he came over to our group. "I have found it, but the name has changed somewhat over the years. In the Bible, it was called Michmash; it is mentioned in Samuel 1, chapters 13 and 14, and tells of a great victory for Jonathan. The extraordinary thing is that we have a parallel situation here. Then, it was the Philistines who were camped high on this hill, and the Israelite Jonathan and his armour bearer found a secret path up to the summit.

"And the garrison of the Philistines went out to the passage of Michmash. Now it came to pass upon a day, that Jonathan the son of Saul said unto the young man that bare his armour, come, and let us go over to the Philistine's garrison, that is on the other side, but he told not his father.

And Saul tarried in the uttermost part of Gibeah under a pomegranate tree which is in Migron: and the people that were with him were about six hundred men;

And between the passages, by which Jonathan sought to go over unto the Philistine's garrison, there was a sharp rock on the one side, and a sharp rock on the other side: and the name of the one was Bozez, and the name of the other Seneh.

The forefront of the one was situate northward over against Michmash, and the other southward over against Gibeah. And Jonathan said to the young man that bare his armour, come, and let us go over unto the Garrison of these uncircumcised: it may be that the Lord will work for us: for there is no restraint to the Lord to save by many or by few. And his armour bearer said unto him, do all that is in thine heart: turn

Thee: behold, I am with thee according to thy heart.

Then said Jonathan, behold, we will pass over unto these men, and we

Will discover ourselves unto them.

If they say thus unto us, tarry until we come to you; then we will stand

Still in our place, and we will not go unto them.

But is they say thus, come up unto us; then we will go up; for the Lord

Hath delivered them into our hand; and this shall be a sign unto us.

And both of them discovered themselves unto the Garrison of the

Philistines; and the Philistines said, behold, the Hebrews come forth out

Of the holes where they hid themselves.

And the men of the Garrison answered Jonathan and his armour bearer,

And said, come up to us, and we will shew you a thing. And Jonathan said unto his armour bearer, come up after me; for the Lord hath

Delivered them into the hand of Israel.

And Jonathan climbed up upon his hands and upon his feet, and his armour

bearer after him; and they fell before Jonathan; and his armour

bearer slew after him.

And that first slaughter, which Jonathan and his armour bearer made,

Was about 20 men, within as it were an half acre of land, which a yoke of

Oxen might plow.

And there was great trembling in the host, in the field, and among all the

People; the Garrison, and the spoilers, they also trembled, and the earth

Quaked; so it was a very great trembling

1 Samuel 14 King James Bible.

There was a stunned silence among us men sitting around the fire after the Major had related the story of Jonathan and Adam's attack on Michmash. You could have heard a pin drop – even on to sand! We could not believe what we were hearing and were stunned to recognise the parallel between our situation three thousand years later and that of the ancient Israelites.

We looked up the passage in our own Bibles. It told us that two men had defeated tens of thousands on the rocky crag less than one mile away from our position right now. We were looking at it. What on earth had really happened here all that time ago?

We all started talking at once in our excitement, and in the end, it was down to the Major to inject some cool common sense.

"We should report this to the Brigadier immediately and recommend that we send some men to the pass to identify where Jonathan climbed the cliff. This could just be the opportunity we are looking for. We all know a full-frontal assault will result in a huge loss of life. I will go and speak to him now."

While he was gone, we were full of questions:

"Why did Jonathan and Adam go on this suicidal mission?"

"Were they assured by God that He would keep them safe and overcome their enemies?"

"Surely they did not think they could overcome all those men?"

"Did God send an earthquake or storm, or both, or was that just an exaggeration?"

"Could it be that the stampeding of thousands of people and horses caused tremors on the earth which could be felt miles away?"

"Why did the enemy start fighting and killing each other? It just doesn't make any sense."

"I hope the Major doesn't send two of us up there and expect the same result!"

"Will the terrain still be the same? Surely it will have changed over time?"

"It is possible winds and storms will have eroded it over the centuries. Or an earthquake could alter the topography of the area."

"My God, that's a long word. What on earth does it mean?"

The Major returned, wearing a big smile. "We are to recce the area and try to find the place. Sergeant, take your men with you. Get into the wadi first, and then try to identify the two rocks, Seneh and Bozez, and work out where Jonathan climbed up to the small patch of land. But first, you need a hot cuppa as you may be away a few hours."

We were camped on high ground, which was possibly the site known as Migron in the Bible. We believed that this was where Saul had camped as he would have had a good view of the enemy up on the higher ground. There was a stone in the ground naming the place as Tel Miriam, but we didn't know its history. The huge upside-down oval bowl of the mountain once known as Michmash was straight ahead of us, a couple of miles away. This was where the enemy was camped. To our left, we could see the small village of Mukhmas about five hundred yards away, just behind the rising ground of the hill where our enemy was. To our right, down below us, we could see the wadi snaking its way between the cliffs and the steep hills on both sides. There was a trickle of water running down the centre of the path, left over from the winter rains. The wadi had been used as a road to Jericho to the east in biblical times.

Dawn was already approaching. We believed the route up the mountain was likely to be guarded, but we did not know how heavily. We set out and walked down our hill towards the wadi. It was still dark, but we got a little light from a thin moon.

The weather was dry, but cold; after our recent experiences, this was a relief for us. The terrible winter rains which had caused us such horrors had left a thin layer of vegetation on the stony ground. I got a strong, almost overpowering scent of rosemary mingled with heather; wildflowers grew here in abundance.

As we reached the bottom of the slope, we had a little difficulty getting into the wadi as we had to climb down a small cliff. We then walked about a mile along the twisting path of the wadi as the cliffs grew on both sides. Gradually, the path narrowed and became more twisted. It was hard to see anything as the narrowness of the passage and the height of the cliffs on both sides reduced the light. The ground was very stony, and so we had to tread carefully.

The cliffs got even higher as we moved forward. We guessed that Seneh and Bozez, the sharp rocks identified in the passage from Samuel, were the two cliffs forming the entrance to the pathway.

The Bible story was beginning to unfold.

Chapter 21

Finding the Pass

The cliffs on either side of us were smooth and steep, making them almost impossible to scale. The path became darker as we walked between them along the winding passage, careful on the stony ground. We wondered how we were going to identify Jonathan's path accessing the heights – if indeed it still existed.

After a few minutes' walk, we saw a shallow climb to our left which could have been shaped by an old watercourse. We were sure this was the right place, the one identified in the Bible. It looked like an easy climb for us, and as we were out of the shadow of the cliffs, a little light helped to guide us.

We walked the first part, and then scrambled over rocks as the path gradually became steeper. The path turned sharply to the left halfway up. We guessed this would lead towards the level ground higher up where Jonathan had first encountered the Philistines. The Bible passage had identified a flat piece of ground near the top where the Philistine outpost was.

I looked up and spotted half a dozen shadowy figures sitting in pairs. Pointing to them, I put a finger up to my lips. Just above them was the level ground of the outpost. We climbed higher and they did not see or hear us.

I decided that we had seen enough, certain that we had found a route for our Army to reach the top. It was now time to climb down and make our way back to the camp.

An hour later, I reported to the Major that we had found the place described in the Bible. "The flat piece of land where Jonathan and his armour bearer climbed up to the Philistines is clearly visible and not too difficult to access. I am sure this is the route we should take. But we need to be aware that there are soldiers protecting the climb. We must deal with them."

"Great work!" the Major replied. "Isn't it extraordinary how the Bible is faithful to the truth, even after three thousand years?" He then hurried off to report the good news to the Brigadier.

In moments, he returned and told us that we would form an advance party, leaving in the early hours of the next morning. We would attain the first strip of land where the Philistines' garrison had been, dispatching the guards on the way. A company of men, roughly two hundred, would be following at a distance and would wait for our all-clear signal. They would have to haul up their weapons, including heavy machine guns and ammunition as our pack animals could not climb the higher part of the hill. The Lewis machine gun alone weighed 30 lbs – not a job to volunteer for. We would all be armed with rifles, ammunition and hand grenades.

The attack would then be launched.

We estimated that the enemy numbered around a thousand on the top of Mukhmas, but there could have been many more. We had read that the Philistines had up to a hundred thousand, but biblical numbers are prone to exaggeration. My team of six men were to silence the guards before they had the chance to raise the alarm. We knew the way, and the company could follow behind at a safe distance.

We would need to kill the guards, of course, but the realities of war had hardened us and none of us had the slightest concern about it. It always amazed me what brutes war had made of us all, but the job had to be done, and the enemy would do the same to us in the blink of an eye.

***

The six of us left camp in the early hours of the next morning. Once again, the air was cold, and the only light we had came from the moon as it drifted from behind the clouds. As we started walking, I experienced a horrible feeling which is difficult to describe. My stomach, head and chest felt as though they were under attack and I thought I was dying. It was the feeling I often got when I was walking into uncertainty and danger, as we had so many times in the past few years. It never got any easier.

My thoughts went to my family and friends back home. Would I ever see them again? Would I see Blighty and London? Would we all sit together for afternoon tea and scones and have a beer in the pub later?

My thoughts drifted to Jenny who lived next door. I'd loved her from the first moment I'd seen her when she moved in. Even though she was several years older than me, it made no difference: Jenny was the girl for me – no doubt about that. There was only one small problem: Jenny was married to the biggest slob in the street, and I could only watch on in horror as he abused her on a daily basis.

Going into action, I always had the same stupid thought that if I closed my eyes and blotted out the present, then this entire nightmare would be over and I would be back at home, but reality crept in soon enough and I forced these useless thoughts out of my mind. Pictures of all the dear friends I had lost over the past months came into my head. Some had been blown to bits, some shot, some had died in terrible agony, some had died of dreadful thirst and some had had their guts ripped out of them. Would I ever see them again? Would we talk about that funny Captain with the inability to say his Rs properly – "You are a fwightful soldier, Sugarman!" – or the pompous portly Colonel who would fall into terrible rages and, while charging up and down, tripped on his shoelaces and tumbled heavily onto his ample front? Would we still have too many pints together and sing at the tops of our voices without a care? Where on earth do all our dear friends and family go when they die? Can we ever hear their familiar voices again, feel their touch, smell their smell and sense their essence? Or are they all gone, dust to dust?

And why have my friends gone before me? Was this my time now? Was I walking towards my death or, even worse, serious disability?

My extreme nervousness caused a knot in my stomach and my whole body felt weak and nauseous. I looked at my hands and could see they were shaking uncontrollably. I was afraid that my knees would give way and I would fall to the ground and be physically sick. My body had suffered so much abuse in the past couple of years; perhaps it was telling me it could not take much more. I dreaded to imagine how much my mind had suffered: probably even more.

Tears were pouring down my cheeks as I felt sorry for myself and all my mates. I struggled really hard to control myself and my emotions, but felt worn out to the very core of my being and my soul. This was the worst attack of nerves I had experienced, and it took an enormous effort to recover my composure and nerve. If my seniors had seen me like this, they would have said, "Get a grip, boy, and be a man" or "Stop behaving like a simpering baby", showing their complete lack of understanding of what was really happening to us.

I wondered if the others ever felt like I did. If they did, they didn't show it. Could they tell how I had been suffering? Did it show on my face? Was there physical evidence of my funk?

I wondered if it hurt to die, or was it a quick release? I am sure it would be better than being maimed. I hoped my friends would put me out of my misery if something terrible ever happened to me; I think we let Herbert down.

We reached the cliffs of Seneh and Bozez in around an hour. The main force would be twenty minutes behind us, but we could not see nor hear them, and that was good news because it meant that the enemy could not either. We peered up the cliff; although we could not see clearly, we knew that the first couple of men were about one hundred yards up.

We walked up silently and slowly. Within minutes, we were able to see the first two men. They were fully relaxed and half dozing, and one had a cigarette dangling out of the corner of his mouth. Leaning back with their feet propped up on a rock, they were clearly not expecting any trouble.

I was leading our group and I was very aware of how important it was to do this quietly and not disturb the men higher up, and certainly not the main enemy force. There was almost no background noise to hide our movements. My heart was thumping and I was sure it could be heard miles away.

I got to within a few feet of the enemy guards and signalled to my friends that I was going to move to the left and climb above them. I waved to Dave to join me; we must have taken only a couple of minutes to get into position, but it seemed like an age.

When we were ready, we dropped a short way on to the men's prone bodies with our knives ready. We dispatched them before they had a chance to cough, let alone cry out.

Signalling a thumbs up to our mates, we climbed higher towards the next two. Time was tight and it would not be long before our main force was due to arrive, and then the game would be up. Unfortunately, I dislodged a small stone and made a slight noise, and both men stood up to look down towards us. We froze and tried to blend into the rock. They called down to us in their language and I guessed they were saying "Who goes there?" or something similar, but they had not spotted us yet.

I decided that we were so close, we would rush them. I signalled this to Dave. Up we went quickly and I grabbed the first man, locking his neck with my right arm and pulling his head back – well, OK, I will spare you the gory details. Dave was doing the same to the other man; they hardly made a sound as they went down.

We waited a couple of seconds, craning our necks up towards the next two men. They had clearly not heard the scuffle. As we were carefully climbing up on all fours towards them, we could hear the main force coming along the pass. We had to move quickly.

Then the most amazing thing happened. One of the men let out a long howl of anguish and threw himself off the ledge above us, plummeting past us headfirst. Just missing us, he crashed into the rocks as he went down, the dreadful howling stopping immediately. I rushed up to silence the other man, but he was so busy crying, he didn't even notice me. I dispatched him with ease.

We never did work out the meaning behind this strange incident; we could only conclude that the two had had a domestic. However, now the cat was out of the bag. Other men on the top of the cliff were looking down towards us and running around in confusion and panic.

Our orders were to wait before moving to the top for the company to catch up with us, and they were now only a few feet away. The sun was rising and we could see very clearly, but then again, so could the enemy. I was getting extremely anxious to take action as I was concerned that we would lose the advantage and the enemy would regroup and attack us, but I stuck to my orders.

We heard our men coming round the pass, and within minutes they had reached our position, led by the Major.

"Well done, chaps. What is happening now?" he whispered.

"Dunno, sir, but I think we need to get up there quickly," I replied, relieved that the Major was now with us. Attack was imminent and there was no time for any more nervous hesitation or reflections.

Chapter 22

The Battle Begins

The Major led us up the last few feet. The enemy soldiers tried to kick us back as our heads appeared over the edge of the plateau, but they did no serious damage. We streamed over the top and began firing into the mass of men who were running in every direction in total confusion; there were perhaps two hundred of them.

I managed to climb on to the flat ground without opposition. We continued firing at the men, but were mystified by the lack of opposition; we had been expecting a real struggle at this stage to get a foothold here. In the noise and panic, the words of the Bible came back to me. Jonathan and his armour bearer had attacked the Philistines in an area "which a yoke of oxen might plough". Yes, this looked about right.

The men were retreating, trying to reach their main Army a few hundred yards away from us, higher up the hill. They hardly retaliated at all as they ran up the hill as fast as they could, speeding towards their friends, screaming and shouting that the British had surrounded them and they would all be killed. At least I think that was what they were saying. They made no effort to fire back as we picked them off quite easily, following them up the large curve of the hill towards the main Turkish Army.

Then another extraordinary thing happened. Hundreds of men turned around and walked towards us, some with their hands high in the air, some with their hands on their heads, some waving white cloths. Many crying uncontrollably, they threw their guns to the ground. We let them walk past us, and then the Major detailed a dozen of our men to lead them towards the outpost. We watched as the captured men were made to sit down and take their boots off, even though there was no danger any of them would run away. Many of them were wailing and crying in despair, and they seemed to be so grateful to be alive and safe. Others were on their knees, either pleading to be spared or thanking us for not killing them. Our men made sure that none was armed, then ordered them to lie down on their backs while more and more miserable and frightened enemy soldiers joined them.

When the numbers started to dwindle, the Major ordered his men to take the prisoners away. They led them, still barefoot, down the slope and lined them up at the foot of the cliff in the wadi. This took some time to complete, and then they waited to see the outcome of the fracas above us. I reckon we had captured around three hundred of the enemy at this stage.

The Major led the rest of us towards the enemy camp over the steep hump of the mound only a few hundred yards away and we fired blindly. Several hundred men were coming towards us; their camp was behind them and their fires were still burning. I could see their tents and horses in the distance. While many were screaming and surrendering, throwing down their weapons, others decided to attack and fired back.

A group of our men had carried our five Lewis guns with ammunition boxes up the mountain and set them up in a secure position on higher ground to our left. It was a good place to fire down on the enemy. Once again, I was grateful that I had not been tasked with carrying the guns up the cliff; the ammunition alone was a crippling weight.

As we took our positions and fired into the mass of the enemy, it soon became apparent that this was not going to be a total walkover. Within minutes, two of our machine gunners were hit, one by a soldier who ran right up to us and chucked a grenade at the gunner to my left and the other from rifle fire. I had to fire almost non-stop as dozens of men kept running towards us with fixed bayonets. We were still outnumbered, at a guess by around five to one, so we had to fight hard to overcome them.

There was no doubt about the single-minded intention of the men charging towards our Lewis guns. They were brave fighters who were determined to throw us off the mountain, but they had never regrouped properly after the initial confusion and there didn't seem to be any clear leadership. There was no time to feel afraid as the three of us were firing like hell, even though we were in danger of being overwhelmed. There must have been fifty men running towards us, some throwing grenades, some firing wildly, others determined to spear us with their bayonets.

One brave man charged towards my machine gun with his bayonet pushed forward, determined to end my life. I had only a few rounds left; I pressed the button and heard the rat-tat-tat of my big gun, instinctively tucking my head down low to give him a smaller target. Even today, I can still see the man with his pale face and huge dark moustache, but most of all, I recall his wild staring eyes. The experience would give me regular nightmares for many years.

He was so close that I thought I could smell his disgusting garlic breath. He was not giving up; he charged to within a yard of where I was standing, firing straight at him. He must have taken dozens of bullets. Just before he reached me, his head flew off his body and the rest of him crashed into me and the gun, knocking the breath out of me as I went sprawling back.

It was a close-run thing. I almost passed out with the shock and fright of the terrible encounter, but I got away with just a few bruises. Pushing his body away, I was shaking as I reloaded the gun as quickly as I could and silently thanked the Lord for my survival.

I continued to fire at the mass of enemy as they kept coming towards me. Our men fought with incredible bravery and determination, and slowly we gained the advantage. In less than an hour, the fight was out of the enemy and the final few hundred held their hands up, their eyes pleading with us not to kill them. They had all thrown down their weapons and some were holding white rags in their hands, waving them to ensure we understood their intention to surrender. I was bathed in sweat from the ordeal and fright from my close shave and now felt totally exhausted, but still I hugged my men, crying in grateful relief.

We led our prisoners back to the cliff and made them climb down to the others barefoot. That was it: we had won the battle and our ordeal was over.

We celebrated the incredible relief of victory and our good fortune that day. I had completely forgotten about my earlier funk, having been totally caught up and involved in the fighting. My pain and fear had gone.

While a medical team arrived at the site to tend to the more seriously wounded, our next task was to count the number of enemy dead for our report. They would be buried later at the place where they had fallen. We were extremely fortunate to have only about a dozen dead and half that number seriously wounded; we were expecting to have many more. I wondered how we'd managed to win so easily.

Someone passed me a water bottle and I drank deeply. Its extraordinary how dry you can get during battle action, but not notice your thirst until the action is over. Then it was time to clear up and head home to our camp.

We stripped down our guns, and then had to carry them to the cliff edge and lower them to the ground. In our exhilaration, we didn't mind at all, and anyway, this was better than carrying them uphill. We then joined the prisoners at the base of the cliff, walking them back to our camp. Now, we had the problem of looking after hundreds of new arrivals at the camp, despite feeling incredibly tired and drained ourselves.

A company was sent to the mountain site to collect food and water and other enemy stores and weapons. There were dozens of their horses to round up and look after, but with the enemy's provisions, we now had enough to feed and water our prisoners and the animals and refresh ourselves.

Most of the enemy were in a dreadful state, a much worse condition than we were. The men were thin and gaunt from a lack of sustenance and their equipment was woeful. But they were simply grateful that their war was over and they could get some desperately needed rest and recuperation.

We still could not believe our good fortune in defeating the enemy with so few losses on our side. When the General came over to visit us at Mukhmas, he was so overwhelmed with our achievements that he called all of us together and delivered an impassioned speech praising our victory. He told us that thanks to our endeavours, the path now lay clear to pursue the enemy to the River Jordan and beyond.

The end of our war was in sight. We were looking forward to finishing the job.

Chapter 23

Memories of Michmash

The following day, a dozen villagers from Mukhmas brought us some slaughtered goats and vegetables to thanks us for routing the Turks and I began to put together a feast. Of course, my friends knew that I had been a trainee chef before the war, but I had made it clear to them that I joined up to fight, not to cook. However, this would be a good time to show off my skills and give them all a treat.

I needed plenty of help, so I detailed a dozen men to light cooking fires and obtain large pots. I detailed another dozen to trade with the villagers for some herbs and spices and more vegetables. Meanwhile, I butchered the goats, separating the meat from the bones and cutting it into bite-sized chunks. I asked the camp cooks to help as plenty of preparation was required.

I had decided to make a spicy stew in a Middle Eastern style, and I hoped that the men could find the appropriate ingredients. I was pleased that they had brought back plenty of rice, which I was going to cook separately, more vegetables, a few onions and loads of fruit, which would give the stew a rich sweetness. There were olives which added to the richness, a flavour that would have been new to many of the men. I also had figs, dates and mangoes, and I added them all, along with coconut milk and flesh.

The villagers supplied many kinds of spices, including cinnamon, turmeric, cumin and saffron as well as some I had never come across before, and herbs including rosemary, coriander, and mint. Hot peppers and garlic helped to give the dish richness and spice.

For the first time in my life, I was the head chef and I thoroughly enjoyed directing dozens of men to do different jobs. I decided then that I would like to go back to my peacetime job and work my way up in the commercial kitchen. This was what I wanted to do, and it was a relief to discover my future path.

The stew grew thicker, richer and more flavourful. I made a big show of tasting each pot and directing where more of this and more of that should be added, ensuring the contents of each pot was slightly different so I could experiment with ingredients and flavours. I then tried samples of the goat meat and discovered it was absolutely delicious: meaty, but tender and full of flavour.

The gravy had thickened into a luscious sauce. The steam and the irresistible aroma wafted over the whole camp and everyone was slavering for a plateful. I directed that every man – there must have been two hundred, and these were really hungry men – have a portion of rice with a good dollop of the stew on top, joking that this was like the feeding of the five thousand. I am sure none of them had tasted anything remotely like this before, but they wolfed it down.

I directed each man to have a second portion, and then a third. One man came back and asked for more twelve times, so we nicknamed him Oliver. At last, the food was all gone, and fortunately all had eaten their fill. Everyone praised me for my miraculous creation, hoisting me onto their shoulders, spinning me round and shouting their compliments. I was the most popular man in the camp for many weeks. Of course, they all begged me to cook more dishes, but I reminded them that I was there to fight, not cook, and went back to my original resolve. On the quiet, though, I took careful note of all the new foodstuffs I had used and decided to source and work with them again after the War.

We had a busy few days looking after our prisoners, and then we sent them back for internment in Jerusalem. They were no longer our problem; now we had the chance for a couple of days' rest before we followed the Turks' main Army. In an impromptu meeting of the God Squaddies, we reviewed the Old Testament story of Michmash and our amazing parallel modern-day experience.

We sat around the fire with our big, comforting mugs of steaming tea, without which I don't think we could have survived, delighted that the Major joined us as he had played the leadership role in our recent success. He began by congratulating us on our bravery, and also our initiative in bringing the Old Testament event to him, and subsequently to our Commanders.

I started the discussion by reading the Bible story aloud once again, starting with 1 Samuel chapter 13 to give the background, and then chapter 14 telling the main story. As I spoke, I pointed towards the places where Jonathan's miraculous success had taken place, starting with our camp which was where King Saul's Army had been based. I pointed to where both the ancient

Philistines and the modern-day Turkish had been strategically encamped on top of the huge mound of Michmash straight ahead of us.

I then waved my arm to the wadi way below us, which went snaking towards Jericho many miles away. We could see the cliffs on either side, but the pass up to the flat piece of land was out of sight, hidden by a turn in the wadi. Behind us lay the small village. We could see why Saul had been tempted to attack the enemy by going through the village, but he would have come face to face with them, which would have been disastrous for the Israelites as the thousands of Philistine chariots would have charged and annihilated them. I talked about Jonathan's clever move, surprising the Philistines by coming up from the so-called inaccessible side and confusing the enemy, who thought that they must be surrounded by Saul's Army.

I told this story in a dramatic voice, speaking slowly and sonorously. I really think that my friends were deeply moved by this, or maybe they just knew me too well; either way, they were very quiet until I had finished the first part of the story. I then reminded them about our own adventure and the extraordinary parallels between the two attacks which happened in the same place with the same result, but three thousand years apart. I asked the group why this had happened and what elements of the stories had been significant in the outcome.

"Why did Jonathan approach the huge Philistine Army with only one man? What did he hope to achieve? Can we look towards a religious element here in that God told him to do this, or is there a more human and practical answer?"

"I think that God protected the Israelites and made all these things happen for them," Dave replied, as ever ready to believe in the influence of God without question. "Look at how He made the sun stand still for a day so that Joshua could defeat the Amorites."

"And He sent down large hailstones which killed more of them than the Israelites did," added Arty.

Bill, as usual, had a more cynical view. "I just don't believe that. Why on earth would God take sides? Men had to fight to win battles and use better tactics than the other side. They had to use the land to its best advantage, and if they were fortunate enough to be helped by the weather, good luck to them. These were real people who had to outsmart the enemy."

Harry agreed with him. "We have had to fight hard against Johnny, and we've lost many of our good men in the process. The tide of the war only started moving in our favour when Bloody Bull took over and changed the way things were done. God never intervened to help us, or them. If He had done so, it would have made a nonsense of the principle of free will. No, the identical outcomes of the two battles of Michmash were down to human resourcefulness."

"Maybe it was the surprise factor," I suggested. "The Philistines just did not expect the Israelites to come from the opposite side as they didn't believe this was possible. They had been looking forward to annihilating them from the front. The element of surprise threw them into disarray and panic."

"I think God created the path especially for Jonathan to access the flat piece of land and then the mountain, just as we did." That was Arty again.

"That's bilge!" Bill snapped. "The land is shaped by weather and earthquakes, not by the finger of God. If He does exist, and I believe He does, He doesn't go round creating pathways for the benefit of His favoured people. That just can't be true.

"I don't want to offend anyone, and we are all entitled to our own beliefs and to practise our religion in peace and freedom – indeed, I believe that this is one of the reasons we are fighting this war. We are freeing the people of Palestine from the heavy yoke of Turkish oppression and the people of Europe from the weight of German dominance. We do this because we believe in self-determination."

"I think there is another factor behind this success." The Major's hypnotic voice and dramatic delivery (better than mine, I must admit!) caused the men to go quiet, wondering what was coming next. "Sound played a significant part. Remember the first skirmish on the flat ground? The noise from that must have hit the wadi on its snaky path, and then bounced back up the cliffs to the enemy higher up. It would have been greatly magnified and hit them from many angles – a truly terrifying experience which seriously disorientated them. They believed that they were being attacked from all sides and got really confused about who was friend and foe."

We all went quiet once again as we digested these words from the Major. He had put his finger on the most fundamental part of the story, and although none of us could prove or disprove his point, we knew he was likely to be right.

It was now time to move on.

Chapter 24

Final Days of War

We spent a couple of days in Jerusalem, and then started the long walk down towards Jericho through the bare, desolate limestone hills. The weather was hot and still, and as we descended closer to the River Jordan, the air became more oppressive.

There were pockets of the enemy in certain strategic places, the first being Talaat-ed-Dumm where we charged Johnny uphill. Johnny was not giving up easily and there was terrible fighting with bad losses on both sides, but we eventually forced him off the hill and he ran back towards the Jordan. We marched on down to the River Jordan, thirteen hundred feet below sea level.

As we climbed down, we saw the mountain of Nabi Musa close to the road on our right. Named after Moses, it was where he is alleged to have been buried, although the Bible suggests it was Mount Nebo which can be seen to the east from the top of Nabi Musa. Either way, this sparked a short discussion that evening among the God Squaddies. Arty thought that we were at the place where

Moses had looked upon the Promised Land for the last time as God did not let him travel there. Dave corrected him and said that Moses did not travel across the River Jordan and had looked over Israel from Mount Nebo.

Then we discussed the Mount of Temptation where Jesus was tempted by the Devil. The mountain is over 900 feet high, and the Major and several other officers had climbed up the far side to see where the enemy were, reporting back to us later that they had seen the fantastic spectacle of the Australian Cavalry, our brave and successful allies, in formation, charging towards the small settlement of Jericho before getting lost from view in the dust. The Major was also excited to have had his first clear view of the Dead Sea and the River Jordan.

The discussions that evening went on to centre around Jericho and the mystery of how the walls had fallen down. Harry thought it was due to the vibrations caused by the noise of the trumpets, while of course Arty and Dave said that God had knocked over the walls. No one could improve on these ideas, so opinion remained divided between the two.

We talked about the importance of the River Jordan in the Bible and how it ran from the Lake of Galilee down to the Dead Sea. John the Baptist had preached and performed baptisms in the river, and it was there that he foresaw the coming of Jesus. In fact, he'd had the honour of baptising Jesus there, but was subsequently taken by the Romans and beheaded by Herod. Harry mentioned that Josephus, a Roman soldier who had witnessed many Biblical events, had written about John the Baptist and described him as a good man who was treated unjustly.

We were extremely excited to be getting our first views of the River Jordan the following day, although the circumstance was not a happy one. Unusually, the river was in full flood and the retreating enemy had destroyed the bridges, so we had to build a new one. Firstly, we had to get volunteers to swim across; although dozens wanted to try, unfortunately, many were drowned before the first man succeeded. In addition to the raging currents, they had the added challenge of the enemy firing at them all the time. But against the odds, our brave men prevailed, and then we could pull a chain across. Later, we managed to carry our machine guns across on a raft. I was very proud to see that Allenby was there to witness this.

We had dreadful times as we travelled east and fought uphill for many miles, climbing steeper and taller mountains than we had seen before. The weather was freezing and wet and the going was very muddy. The sides of the wadis were so steep that we often had to lower our horses and mules down by rope.

Our objective was to capture Amman and we climbed 3,500 feet to reach it. We fought for three days while suffering from extreme hunger and distress, and many of our men died of exposure. Fortunately, the powers that be decided we should abandon the attempt, and over a period of time we travelled back and crossed the Jordan, where we camped for several weeks.

Then we were ordered to march back to the west coast. The plan was to launch a surprise attack on the enemy on the western plain and convince them that we had left the main part of our Army by the Jordan. A skeleton troop created camouflage camps with horses made of blankets and hundreds of tents, then raised clouds of dust by driving lorries around in circles, firing captured enemy guns into the air. The enemy were convinced we were still there and had no idea we had escaped to the west. Further east, TE Lawrence led the Arabs in disrupting the enemy and destroying their railway lines and weapon dumps, so we were not bothered by them.

In the meantime, many thousands of us gathered on the maritime plain in the west. My men were part of the force used to break open a gap in the enemy lines to let the cavalry through. We won the final battle within thirty-six hours, taking possession of the northern part of the country and chasing the enemy up to Damascus and beyond. They surrendered at the end of October that year.

Our only priority now was to get home. We had been in the Holy Land for one year and away from home for three, but there were long delays in shipping us back. After his success as our Leader, Allenby had to face the indignity of the men coming close to rioting as they waited for weeks in Egypt.

We God Squaddies had plenty of time to chat about our experiences and the biblical places we had visited. But there was one more place we were desperate to visit and we were delighted to learn that we would be posted near to the legendary Sea of Galilee to assist with guarding some enemy prisoners. Well, we just couldn't believe our good luck. These waters had witnessed so many biblical events.

I will never forget the day we arrived at the lake's shores, amazed at its beauty. A warm sun welcomed us, and even our guarding work wasn't too taxing. In our element, we God Squaddies talked long into the night about this special place.

"It's exactly as the Bible describes," Arty said. "Those fishing boats over there, they probably look as they did two thousand years ago. Do you think those lads would take us out in one for a day's fishing?"

"Well, they can't expect us to walk on the water," replied Bill. "How did Jesus do that, or was it just an illusion?"

We found a tiny church next to the Sea which housed an extraordinary rock formation. We were told this was where Jesus had cooked fish for the disciples, and there were small seats and a flat pan for cooking carved into the stone. This was a very special place for us, and we spent a few moments of silence while we imagined the event taking place.

The views from the hills behind us, overlooking the sea, were extraordinary. A local farmer explained that this was the site of the Horns of Hattin, where Saladin had won a famous victory over the Crusaders in 1187. This was also the place, we were told, where Jesus had delivered his Sermon on the Mount and fed the five thousand.

"That was even more of a miracle than walking on water," Dave observed. "How could he do that with just five loaves and two fishes?"

"Probably just another illusion. You've got to take a lot of what the Bible says with a pinch of salt," Bill replied with his usual cynicism.

"Nonsense! Every word of the Bible is true. It was written by God!"

These were precious times for us. Unlike our comrades, we God Squaddies were grateful for the delays in getting home.

Chapter 25

Homecoming

Eventually, we did get home, coming back as different people. Even my own family didn't recognise me; I had lost weight and looked more lined and much older. But it was wonderful to be back in the Smoke, as we Londoners affectionately refer to our hometown.

One of my first priorities was to find out how Jenny was. Her slob of a husband had been carried back from the Western Front after he'd suffered from a gas attack. For years, I had fervently wished to get him out of the way, but not like this. Even that devil did not deserve to suffer as he did, gasping for breath for three weeks before he finally died in terrible pain with his lungs burned out.

But the outcome for me was a happy one. Jenny was free to become my wife.

Many of my friends remained unemployed for a few years, but I was very fortunate to get my old job back at the Goring Hotel. Over the years, I worked my way up the ranks in the kitchen until I was extremely proud to become Head Chef. The work was always incredibly hard with long hours, but the Goring family looked after us really well, and when I finally retired, they paid me a good pension.

All the chefs in the main London hotels knew each other and we were a close-knit bunch. We used to meet regularly and share ideas, which was a great way to increase our knowledge of food, flavour and nutrition. We all had to keep trying new dishes to keep our guests happy, and to attract new people, of course, so it was important to get feedback and continually improve. I made some new dishes with the herbs and spices I had used in the East.

I would nag my commis, "Taste your dish, season your food and taste it again until you have got it right. Make sure hot dishes are always served piping hot."

The best and most enjoyable part of my job was the pastry work and I could have quite happily been a pâtissier full time. My speciality was working with sugar. I used to take great pride in designing models of animals and flowers in all different colours, either as a show piece in the lounge or as a decoration for a celebration cake, culminating in a full page spread in the *Caterer and*

Hotelkeeper with photographs of my divine works of art. The article was headlined "Sugarman's Sweet", but I would have preferred "Sugarman's Brilliant"! I was very proud of my skills, which took me many years to perfect until no one could equal them.

I used to get invited to chefs' homes where they were proud to serve food filched from their kitchens and wines specially bottled for the Dorchester or Savoy. I did not approve of this practice and never allowed it in my kitchen, but of course, I didn't refuse the delicious offerings either.

I cooked for every member of the Royal Family on many occasions and got to know their favourite foods. I especially liked it when Elizabeth, the Duchess of York came to visit. She was so lovely to everyone and was known as the smiling Duchess. She was, of course, married to Prince Albert, our future King George VI, and eventually became known as the Queen Mother.

The Duchess of York loved her food and drink, and her favourites were either Tipsy Tart with a whiff of brandy or Soufflé Rothschild with cherries and plenty of double cream. She also loved my omelettes. I would make another of her favourites,

Oeufs Drumkilbo, every day just in case she called in. Made with hard-boiled eggs, pieces of lobster and a few prawns mixed with mayonnaise, diced tomatoes and copious amounts of Tabasco sauce and anchovy essence, it became a very popular dish for many other guests as well.

The Duchess enjoyed all her food with a variety of drinks, but I am far too diplomatic to go into any detail about that! I am sure that with her good appetite, she will live to a great age.

***

Jenny and I now have grandchildren from our eldest son, Alfred, and I have retired from my work. Very sadly, our younger two sons were killed in World War II. They were just boys and far too young to experience such horrors and suffering. I don't think Jenny and I will ever get over this; we are still utterly desolate, and I don't want to say any more. Instead, we dote on our three grandchildren, Mary, Isabel and Jack, and this softens our never-ending grief ever so slightly.

To this day, I cannot understand how World Leaders managed to get involved in an even bigger war just twenty years after the end of the Great War. You would think after those terrible years that every effort would have been made to prevent this from ever happening again, but no, we stumbled into more years of hell with millions more lives lost and ruined, and families destroyed.

But as I sit in my favourite chair, I often recall my great adventure in Palestine. We God Squaddies promised each other that we would meet up in London frequently so that we could continue our Bible readings and discussions and talk about the extraordinary adventures we had experienced and the terrible losses we had suffered. And whenever we do so, our favourite subject is always Michmash and the part we played in its miracle. Unfortunately our meetings became less frequent until we met no more.

Picture1: The author in front of the battlefield

Picture 2: The small town of Michmash of the Bible. Now called Mukhmas.

Picture 3: The route Jonathan took from Geba.

Picture 4: The Photographer Georgia Margetts

Picture 5: Note the path twisting towards the two cliffs Seneh and Bozez, leading to the secret route to the higher ground mentioned in the Bible

Picture 6: The higher ground behind the town is where the enemy was gathered.

Bibliography

Gilbert, V *The Romance of the Last Crusade* (D Appleton and Company, 1923)

Halkin, H *A Strange Death* (Public Affairs, a member of Perseus Books Group, 2005)

Hoffmeier, JK *The Archaeology of the Bible* (Lion Hudson, 2008)

Kenyon, KM *Archaeology in the Holy Land* (Ernest Benn Limited, 1979)

Murphy-O'Connor, J *The Holy Land: An Oxford archaeological guide from earliest times to 1700* (Oxford University Press, 1992)

Pegler, M *British Tommy 1914–18* (Osprey Publishing Ltd, 1996, illustrated by Mike Chappell)

Massey WT *How Jerusalem Was Won: Being the record of Allenby's campaign in Palestine*. Project Gutenberg free e-book, www.gutenberg.org/ebooks/10098

Thompson JA *The Bible and Archaeology*. (William B Eerdmans Publishing Co, 1982)

Woodward, DR *Forgotten Soldiers of the First World War* (Tempus Publishing Limited, 2007)

Nigel Messenger is also the author of *Doctors at War*, *Megiddo, The Battles for Armageddon*, and *From Eden to Babylon*.

Doctors at War

The Great War is raging across the world and the British are fighting with their allies against the Macedonians.

In the hospitals of Malta and Salonika, two dedicated doctors are locked in an ongoing battle of their own. One, an active Suffragette trained in Edinburgh, faces a daily fight for status and respect at a time when lady doctors were despised and mistrusted. The other trained in The Royal College of Surgeons in Dublin and nearby hospitals. Both are strongly opinionated and passionate about their calling; a clash of personalities is inevitable. However, love flourishes in the most adverse of conditions – the two doctors go on to set up not one but two practices in London, as well as welcoming a daughter into the world.

As time goes by, war also impacts on the lives of the doctors' descendants. Told from the point of view of various family members, the action leads the reader from the turbulent world of London during the Blitz to the code breaking genius of

Bletchley Park, from the tense Battle of the Atlantic to the terrible Battle of Kohima.

Megiddo, the Battles for Armageddon

Three historic and portentous adventures help shape the remarkable men of the twentieth century.

Megiddo, the Armageddon of the Bible – three momentous battles took place near this ancient settlement in Palestine. Docker Nat Sullivan fights under Allenby during the campaign in the First World War and has vivid dreams of fighting with Richard the Lionheart in the Third Crusade and with the Biblical Deborah, probably one of the greatest generals of all time.

Nat returns to the docks and rises through the Union ranks to become assistant to the political giant and statesman Ernest Bevan, General Secretary of the TUC. Nat, now a Labour MP, follows Ernest as he rises in power during and after World War Two.

From Eden to Babylon

A filthy barge arrives in Basra full of near-dead soldiers, wounded, starved and dehydrated without basic care and medicine, after the British surrender at the battle of Kut. An officer and his team take the poor men off the barge and onto a steamer heading for Bombay, and then by train to a hospital in the cooler Northern India.

He recognises one gravely wounded man who had saved his life in South Africa in the horrendous Boer War some years before. When this man's sister travels to India from England to nurse him back to health, she falls for his rescuer.

The World War I action takes place in Mesopotamia, India, Arabia and South Africa and follows the adventures of a family who work and fight together, and finally reunite at a family wedding.

About the Author

Nigel Messenger has spent a lifetime working in the Hospitality Industry and now has his own consultancy company. He has also worked for and supported the Poppy Factory, which provides employment support to wounded, injured and sick veterans, for almost thirty years.

Apart from his family, Nigel has two major passions – cricket and history. He says, "Teaching history in schools can be very boring for the poor recipients. People remember and relate to stories rather than dates, and my interest is trying to describe the effect historical events had on ordinary men and women and how they coped and survived."

Nigel has written four books about World War I in the Middle East. Book 4 also covers events in World War II. His last two books were inspired by the experiences of his family members in various parts of the world.

"They were not heroes, but ordinary people and families who carried out their duties often under the most extraordinary conditions and deprivation."

Nigel lives in Cheltenham with his family and is a proud member of the Alliance of Independent

Authors. He has made several visits to Israel and Jordan and has cycled the length and breadth of both countries twice. Here's what he has to say about a visit to Michmash a few years ago:

"My wife, granddaughter and I visited Michmash, or Mukhmas as it is now known, in the West Bank and I walked up to the town square to ask where the battlefield was. A group of elderly Arabs surrounded me with curiosity and asked which battle I was referring to.

"'The battle of Michmash in the Old Testament, recorded in Samuel.'

"One replied, 'Well, I may look old to you, but I can assure you that I'm not that old!'

"'Ah well, there was another battle here in 1918,' I said.

"'I'm not that old either!' he responded.

"It was a fun moment, but unfortunately, no one had heard of the place or the events. But as we were driving away, I recognised the topography of the battlefield and we spent an hour walking the site. Our driver became extremely distressed, advising us that we were in grave danger, and we had no choice but to leave early. However, we managed to take some photos, some of which I have displayed in this book.

"My burning ambition is to return and explore the site in more detail."

Nigel Messenger

ACKNOWLEDGEMENTS

"My very grateful thanks are due to my Editor Alison Jack for improving my words and texts immeasurably. She has colossal patience and attention to detail. My book is far better thanks to her valuable efforts.

Many have praised the book cover design by Jason Conway of The Daydream Academy, and I think it is a masterpiece! Thank you, Jason.

I am most grateful to members of the Cheltenham Authors Alliance who have been very helpful and generous in their advice and encouragement.

And of course, to my dear and very patient wife, Maura, who heroically puts up with me. I read paragraphs of my books to her enabling her to doze peacefully on the sofa."

Lightning Source UK Ltd.
Milton Keynes UK
UKHW012349110821
388670UK00002B/112